THE ART OF
Baking Bread

THE ART OF
Baking Bread

What You Really Need to Know to Make Great Bread

BY

Matt Pellegrini

Skyhorse Publishing

All Rights Reserved. No part of this book may be reproduced in any manner without the express written consent of the publisher, except in the case of brief excerpts in critical reviews or articles. All inquiries should be addressed to Skyhorse Publishing, 307 West 36th Street, 11th Floor, New York, NY 10018.

Skyhorse Publishing books may be purchased in bulk at special discounts for sales promotion, corporate gifts, fund-raising, or educational purposes. Special editions can also be created to specifications. For details, contact the Special Sales Department, Skyhorse Publishing, 307 West 36th Street, 11th Floor, New York, NY 10018 or info@skyhorsepublishing.com.

Skyhorse® and Skyhorse Publishing® are registered trademarks of Skyhorse Publishing, Inc.®, a Delaware corporation.

Visit our website at www.skyhorsepublishing.com.

10 9 8 7 6 5 4 3 2 1

Library of Congress Cataloging-in-Publication Data is available on file.

ISBN: 978-1-61608-537-7

Printed in China

To my bread tasters:
Mom, Andy, Jill, Mary, Sally,
Dan, Brandy, Ally, Appie, and
Momo (as long as the bread had butter on it).
I hope it wasn't too much trouble.

CONTENTS

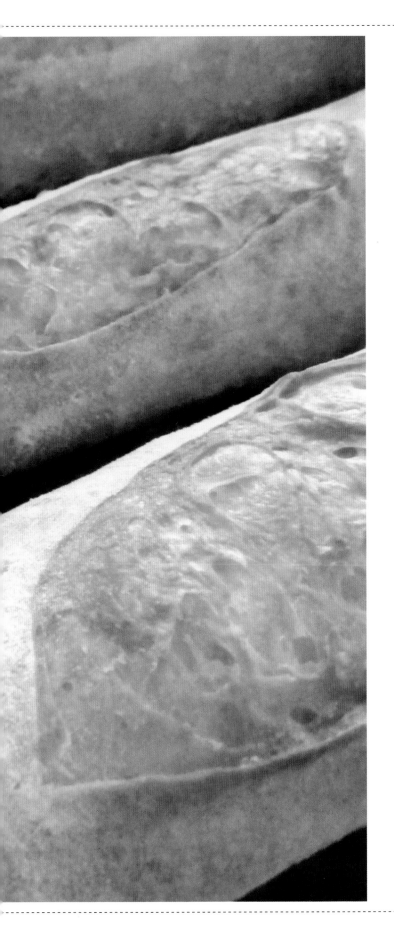

The goal of this book is simple: I want everyone with the desire to bake bread to be able to read the instructions contained within and create a bakery-quality loaf of bread on your first try—no matter if this is the first or fiftieth attempt at doing so. I fully appreciate the monumental challenge inherent in this objective; however, at the same time, I recognize that this goal is wholly achievable so long as one key ingredient is present: detailed, step-by-step instructions with plenty of photos that describe and depict not only what to do but what you should be thinking about, anticipating, smelling, feeling, and ultimately, tasting as you bake great bread.

My conviction for creating this book arose because of what I encountered during my pursuit to create the best of the best *pain di mie,* baguettes, *ciabatta, focaccia,* brioche, and challah, along with many others varieties of bread. I had read the classics, which are nothing less than an absolute necessity for any baker aspiring to advance her skills. But aside from that, those same books are almost universally geared toward individuals with an already existing base of knowledge. And all too often the descriptions and instructions, along with a general lack of photos and other visuals that make life for the beginner easier, left out certain steps or explanations that play an enormous role in the baking process for the beginner. For the new student, these often overlooked and underdiscussed steps are, in fact, some of the most important to a complete understanding of the topic or discipline at hand.

As a result, I was forced to continuously refer to many books at once and scour the Internet to find out exactly what the authors meant or try to figure out what the authors omitted from their text. In the end, I was able to piece together the puzzle to create bakery-quality bread in my home, but not without a great number of overproofed, underbaked, and flat-out disastrous loaves, which necessarily included more than a healthy dose of frustration and disappointment—and to be completely honest, some not-so-repressed hostility toward the so-called experts.

But as with many things in life, out of tragedy comes triumph. And so blossomed the idea for this book—much like a perfectly prepared *boule* springs up in the oven during its first few minutes of baking, expanding to its full, magnificent capacity,

bringing to life the baker's signature score. My intent is to demonstrate *in one single book* what you'll need to know to make and master great bread now, without having to play musical books with what's already been written. Then once you digest all of this, you'll be able to utilize books from the great bakers, taking full advantage of their expertise and foresight in advancing bread baking and moving your bread baking to the next spectacular level.

And by the time your first loaf has completely cooled on the rack and you take that first bite, you will no doubt experience a state of bread-induced nirvana that, if you're anything like me, will become contagious. I must warn you though, as there is one downside to all of this: You'll need to find a steady group of family, friends, or even strangers to help you eat all the bread you'll produce, because I can guarantee that you won't be able to stop after creating just one impeccable loaf.

With that in mind, I wish you many smiles, endless clouds of flour in the air, and crispy crusts galore as you venture forth on your journey of creating world-class bread whenever you want, wherever you want.

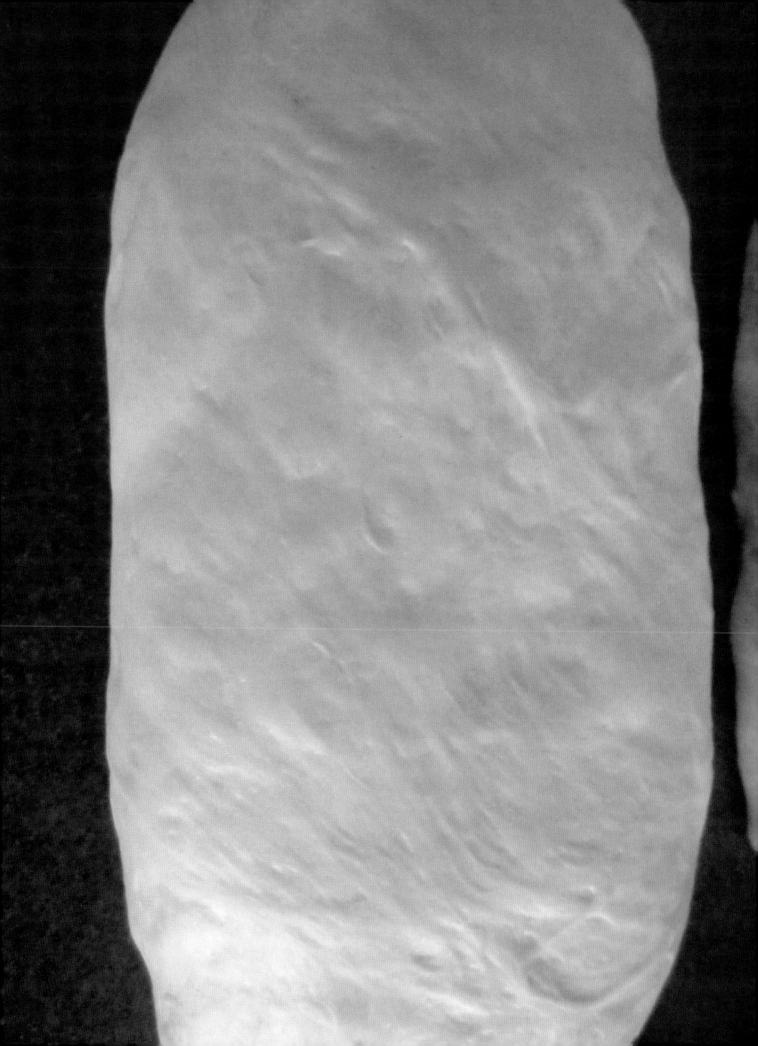

Ingredients and Equipment

WHEN I FIRST BEGAN BAKING BREAD, I'D quickly look at the ingredients and make a list in my head of the tools I'd likely need, then jump right into mixing without much thought for what the ingredients did or how the equipment helped—or hurt—the bread baking process. I had no idea that the ingredients and equipment made a difference in the end result, and more to my surprise, none of the cookbooks I was using said all that much about them either. It wasn't until I opened a cookbook on professional baking that I realized my mistake. It didn't take more than a few minutes of flipping through the pages to realize just how important— and scientifically technical—using the right ingredients and equipment are to the bread-baking process. I learned in rapid fashion that in the world of baking, knowledge truly is power.

The fact of the matter is that the right ingredients and equipment are the building blocks upon which every other instruction in this book—and all books, for that matter—are based. I cannot overstate the importance of understanding the nature of the ingredients and tools that are part and parcel of the baking process. If you follow in my footsteps, there's no doubt you'll have more than a few of those "a-ha moments" as you delve into this world.

Ingredients

Flour

Like me, you might have once thought, or continue to think, that flour is flour, and that's that. This flawed thinking could not be farther from the truth. Flour is a science unto itself, and the sooner you come to terms with that as a baker, the closer you will be to producing bakery quality bread on your first attempt.

Although flour can come from many sources, such as rice and potatoes, we will be concentrating our discussion on wheat flour, mainly because it serves as the basis for the vast majority of the centuries-old recipes that we're all so familiar with—from baguettes to brioche.

And although it would be easy to become lost in the agricultural science behind wheat flour, we're going to avoid that and concentrate on the one factor that will impact your bread baking the most: gluten content.

Gluten is a two-component protein, composed of glutenin, which provides elasticity, and gliadin, which adds extensibility, or resistance to stretching. These two components work together in balance to create structure within the dough, which in turn provides the framework for gas to become trapped within the dough. The internal structure and the gas that is trapped within the dough produce—if everything else falls into place—what bakers call a nice "crumb." The crumb is simply the technical name for the inside of the bread, as opposed to the "crust," which is the outside of the loaf of bread. For our purposes, we will focus on gluten content for the type of flour most commonly used in bread baking: bread flour.

By definition, bread flour possesses a gluten content of around 11%–13%. (For the sake of comparison, cake flour contains has 6%–9% gluten content and all-purpose flour is in the vicinity of 8%–12%). Bread will certainly rise and bake with lesser

LEHI ROLLER MILLS

USE TURKEY RED FLOUR · PEACOCK FLOUR STANDS FOR QUALITY

SINCE 1906

Certified
High Gluten Flour
-Organic-
50 lbs Net

Lehi Roller Mills Co. Inc.

If you cannot determine the gluten content of the flour from the labeling on the package, don't be shy; call the flour mill. If it's a quality organization, the customer service representatives will be able to provide you with everything you wanted to know and more about their products.

The large and glossy holes here are made possible by gluten.

gluten content flour, but the rise may be so slight that the baking part produces something more akin to a flatbread than to a nicely raised loaf of Italian bread.

It is important to note that whole wheat flour possesses a very high gluten content—14%–16%. However, the hulls contained in the whole wheat flour tend to sever gluten strands, making the gluten less effective. Because of this, when whole wheat bread is made, a portion of the flour is typically bread flour, or at a minimum, all-purpose flour. The addition of the higher-gluten (and hull-less) bread or all-purpose flour helps to preserve the integrity of the gluten in the overall recipe. This will aid in creating volume in the loaf, along with a lighter crumb, or internal structure. Without out the addition of the non-whole wheat flour, the loaf of bread will be ultra dense.

Not all bread flour is created equal. Although bread flour is the term used for the higher gluten flour used in bread baking, the percentage of gluten is not standardized across different brands.

Yeast

Yeast is the giver of life to bread. Without it you'll have nothing but a concoction of flour, water, and salt that, when baked, will taste like nothing more than a random concoction of flour, water, and salt. Sure, it will have nutrients and could keep you alive in a pinch, but let's be clear, it's not what most of us picture in our minds when we envision bread just out of the ovens at the bakery.

What is yeast? It's a microorganism that's part of the fungi family and contains over a dozen enzymes that help to reduce carbohydrates into useable forms. Yeast produces carbon dioxide and alcohol. The former inflates the internal structure created from the gluten while the latter burns off during baking. Temperature, moisture, oxygen, and the nutrient source all determine how well the yeast will thrive. (Although I could devote an entire chapter, if not book, to the physiology of yeast, further elaboration would most likely cause you to close this book and use it as a wedge under a wobbly table or chair. If you'd like to learn more about yeast, I suggest obtaining a good book on food science, which will provide you with a more thorough explanation.)

Yeast can be purchased in three varieties: fresh, active, and instant.

Fresh yeast is preferred by many old-school bakers who started their careers with fresh yeast—because it was the only type available—and continue to tout its superiority to this day. There are many newer bakers who subscribe to this position as well. For the home baker, though, it's somewhat of a nuisance to deal with because of its shorter shelf life and the fact that its ability to produce gas diminishes with age. Because of this, the other two types of yeast are more suited for the home baker.

Store your yeast in an airtight container to maximize its life.

Active dry yeast is yeast in a granular form. Active dry yeast must be combined with water, or proofed, to activate it prior to adding it to the rest of the ingredients. The reason for this is due to the fact that active dry yeast is coarse in texture, so if it were simply added to the rest of the ingredients, it would not dissolve properly. Proofing it with water allows the yeast to dissolve so that it can do what it's supposed to do in the dough. Plus, it's a great way to check to see if the yeast is still usable.

Although bakers worldwide will argue over this point until time eternal, instant dry yeast, which is the finest in texture of all the yeasts, is the yeast of choice for our purposes mainly because of its ease of use. It stores well in the freezer and can last up to several months. More important, it can be added directly to the flour rather than having to proof it beforehand (although you can proof this type in water prior to adding to the rest of the ingredients if it makes you feel more confident). The reason it does not need to be proofed is because it is finer in texture than active dry yeast so it readily dissolves in the dough. On top of this, and largely as a result of advances in food manufacturing, the quality of instant dry yeast is high and works as well as the other two types with much less fuss.

Converting Active to Instant Dry Yeast in a Recipe: Since recipes calling for fresh yeast are rare (and it's hard to come by in a store), here's how to convert a recipe between active and instant dry yeast if you have one on hand but a recipe calls for the other. To convert from active to instant, multiply the active yeast amount by .75 (e.g., 12 grams active yeast x .75 = 9 grams of instant yeast). To convert from instant to active yeast, multiply the instant yeast amount by 1.33 (e.g., 12 of instant yeast x 1.33 = 15.96 (round up to 16) grams of active yeast).

Salt

Salt serves four purposes in bread baking: one, it adds flavor (just don't overdo it); two, it helps to prevent yeast from blooming out of control (although once dissolved and dispersed throughout the dough, it's impact on yeast development is reduced); three, it aids in retaining the quality of the bread (it's a wonderful preservative—think salt cod!); and four, it helps to strengthen gluten (hooray, gluten!). For these reasons, it's essential that salt be included in the bread-baking equation.

With its importance established, it's prudent to discuss the different types of salt that can be used. There are two choices for most people: granular iodized sea salt or kosher salt. Both will achieve the desired result, but because the sea salt is much finer, it will distribute much more easily within the dough. Because of this, all of the recipes in this book will use sea salt. But if you are partial to kosher salt, then by all means use it.

Water

Let's face it: bread would not exist without water. In fact, it serves three major, and indispensible, purposes: One, It's required for gluten to form; two, it dissolves other ingredients (i.e., yeast, salt, sugar, etc.); and three, it's necessary for yeast fermentation.

There are two main concerns when it comes to water. The first is that when possible, every baker should use filtered water. For the professional, high-volume baker, this is a difficult, and if attempted, extremely costly, endeavor. But for the home baker, there is little reason not to use filtered water in the bread-baking process. Certainly, it may not be always possible to taste a difference if filtered or unfiltered water is used, but from a mental perspective, isn't it reassuring to know that you've done all you could to remove as many impurities from your water source as possible. More specifically, though, is the fact that heavily chlorinated water may impede the development of necessary microorganisms in natural leavens like sourdough. Filtering will help to deter this.

Another way to avoid overchlorination is to leave water to sit overnight in a container; this causes chlorine to disperse, thus alleviating the problem.

> Very hard water may retard yeast activity and gluten development, while soft water may cause dough to be overly sticky.

> For the sake of economy, don't use bottled water. Purchase a pitcher-filter, use one of the spigot mounted ones, or if you happen to have a refrigerator equipped with one, draw your water from there. It will save you money that you can better spend on purchasing high-quality flour, eggs, olive oil, and other ingredients.

But beyond the world of filtration, the amount of water in a recipe, which for most breads ranges from 66%–75% or more by weight, determines the quality of the crumb—i.e., big holes versus little ones as well as texture. On top of that, water is essential in the creation of steam emanating from the dough, which helps to produce a wonderful crust. Those are tough arguments to overcome.

Sugar

As much as I love sugar, I do realize that it has its place in bread baking, and that place is rather limited. In fact, it most often finds its home in what is called enriched dough—dough that incorporates fat or sugar in its recipe; however, other dough sometimes utilizes it in rather small amounts.

Sugar serves two main purposes. It is used to sweeten dough, and it can add color to the crust. However, the latter is not as straightforward as it might appear. In order to achieve the proper degree of browning, a fine balance must exist between too little and too much sugar. In fact, sugar's impact on the color of the crust occurs when the

Pain de Mie, one type of bread that benefits from sugar.

total sugar content in the recipe is between 5%–10% by weight. And because of its effect on browning the crust, dough containing sugar must be baked at lower temperatures—generally 350°F–375°F—than dough that does not contain sugar. If you bake it at a higher temperature, the top of the crust will brown before the loaf is fully baked, and the bottom of the loaf may burn.

Beside reducing oven temperature, another way to avoid burning the bottom of a sugar-enriched loaf of bread is to bake it on a sheet pan. This will help to insulate the dough and keep its temperature in the right range to avoid burning.

While some claim that sugar is a source of food for yeast, this is not justified. As it so happens, adding too much sugar can reduce yeast activity, and yeast obtains most of its nutrition from the sugar content of the flour in which it's been incorporated.

You have two choices when it comes to which sugar to use: granulated white sugar or cane sugar. The granulated sugar is much finer than the cane sugar for the most part. However, the flavor of the cane sugar is better. The downside to the cane sugar is that because it is coarser than granulated sugar, it doesn't dissolve as readily. However, in my opinion, the taste is so much better that it trumps the dissolving issue.

As with all ingredients, use organic products when possible. Sure, you may not taste the difference, but isn't it reassuring to know that the quality of your ingredients matches the quality—and quantity—of the effort you're expending to create the bread? Plus, there's no question that it's healthier. Enough said.

Fat

Fat, like sugar, is most often found in enriched dough; however, just like with sugar, it is used in smaller amounts in other types of dough. Fat, in the form of butter, oil, lard, egg yolks, etc., helps to increase bread volume by improving gas retention in the dough, aids in tenderizing the crumb, and acts as a preservative once the dough is baked. It also is a tremendous flavor enhancer, adds nutritional value, and if egg yolks are brushed on top of a loaf of bread, as is common with breads like brioche and challah, it helps to impart color to the crust. (Just like with sugar, you'll need to lower the oven temperature.)

Brioche after scaling. The golden color comes from the large percentage of butter incorporated into the dough.

Milk

Milk serves several purposes in bread baking: it adds moisture, it increases nutritional value, and when brushed on the surface of the dough, it helps to caramelize the crust. However, there's a catch to using milk. If you are going to incorporate milk in yeast-based bread, you must heat the milk to above 190°F (and then let it cool down) before adding it to the rest of the ingredients. Doing so will cause serum protein in the milk, which has a negative impact on gluten development, to break down. This will allow the gluten to develop to its full potential. But there is another option if you don't want to heat the milk. Instead, use dry milk and replace the liquid component of the milk with some of the water from the recipe. Problem solved.

Equipment

Although the right equipment does not a recipe make, having the right items on hand can definitely make life easier in the home bakery. And the fact is that it's highly likely that if you cook or bake at home, you already own most of the equipment you'll need to produce high-quality bread in the comfort of your own kitchen. On top of that, the items that you may not have and will need to purchase are not expensive when compared to much of the equipment necessary to cook fine-dining-quality meals. This frugality fits perfectly in line with what

Despite the fact that bread has in recent years become a meal in itself, it was historically a way to fill the belly with little stress on the pocketbook. There's no reason that the equipment to produce the same should somehow require you to take out a second mortgage on your house.

bread baking should be—getting a lot for very little.

But regardless of cost, having the proper equipment, understanding its value, and knowing how to use it will go a long way toward helping you create those picture-perfect and delightfully tasty loaves of bread you desire.

Ideally, here's what you need:

Scale

The scale is by far the most important piece of equipment that a baker can own. Anyone who tells you otherwise—and I'm going out on a limb here—is a fool. Yes, a fool, and I don't say this lightheartedly.

There's a very good reason for my assertion. Scales give bakers accuracy and consistency. There is absolutely no way that you can measure—with a measuring cup, spoon, or otherwise—precisely the same amount of any one ingredient

(and some are worse than others) every single time you intend to do so. The reason is because measuring with cups and spoons measures volume while measuring on a scale measures weight.

Depending on whether you have a heavy or light hand in the flour bag, the difference in the amount of flour could be as much as an eighth cup. If this doesn't sound like a lot, consider that if your recipe called for eight cups of flour. With a heavy hand, you could actually be putting an extra cup in the flour. The opposite holds true with a light hand. Also keep in mind that flour, and other ingredients, are compacted during packaging and transportation, which further complicates this issue.

Now that it's clear that weighing ingredients is the way to go, the question then becomes what unit of measurement is

The importance of weighing can also be illustrated with the type of salt you use. When you compare granulated sea salt to kosher salt, sea salt is fine while kosher salt is much larger in size. This means that when you measure out a volume amount (i.e., teaspoon, tablespoon, etc.) of sea salt versus kosher salt, more sea salt will be in the measuring spoon than with the kosher salt. Because of this, it's easy to comprehend how the weight difference between a tablespoon of sea salt and kosher salt could be 10 percent or more off. Extracting 10 percent of any one item from a recipe is going to result in exponentially less than perfect results.

best to use: grams or ounces. I, along with most professional bakers, prefer grams because you can monitor the amount in smaller increments—there are 453.59 grams in a pound whereas there are only sixteen ounces in the same quantity—thus making measuring more precise. If you're getting the idea that precision is a critical component of bakery-quality bread baking, then you're right on track to creating a wonderful loaf on your first try.

> If a recipe instructs you to use a certain volume of water (i.e., cups, ounces, or milliliters), measure the water once then weigh it and record the weight. That way the next time you decide to make the recipe, you can just weigh the water. It will be quicker and more accurate.

The best device for measuring grams is a digital scale. The old-school balance scales may look nice and are wonderful to use, but they cost hundreds of dollars, which makes them impractical for the home baker. For that reason, purchase a digital scale, but make sure that the digital scale has a "tare" weight function on it. Tare weight is, in the simplest terms, the weight of an empty container. Here's why it matters. If you simply place a bowl on a scale and add an ingredient, the scale will weigh the ingredient *and* the bowl, so you'll end up with less of your ingredients. By using the tare weight function—which is typically nothing more than the push of a button—the weight of the bowl is zeroed out, or subtracted from the total weight, so that the scale is then only measuring the weight of the ingredient. As a result, you'll have an accurate measurement.

Measuring Devices

Because we'll be weighing all of our ingredients, there is no need to amass measuring cups and spoons. But you will need something to scoop ingredients—mainly flour—out of its bag. There's not much to say about this topic other than to use something that is easy to handle and does the job at the same time. In other words, don't use a teacup to gather five pounds of flour.

Also, if you come across recipes that require you to measure out a volume of water, which is more common than not, purchase a measuring device that has the smallest gradations possible. This means that it is better to have a container that provides measurements every ten milliliters rather than every one hundred. It simply provides for more accuracy.

Bowls

Since all of the techniques and recipes in this book, as well as a good portion of artisan bread-baking books (including those contained within the reference guide),

take advantage of mixing by hand rather than using an electric mixer, a bowl takes on more importance than you might expect. We'll be using them to mix and bulk ferment, two ultraimportant stages of bread making, so it helps to have something that works well in front of you.

The material the bowl is made of is not as critical as its size. The general rule is to make sure that you have the right size of bowl for the job at hand. For mixing, this means that it is best to use a bowl that is larger than what you think you need. There is nothing more frustrating—or tough on the hands—than trying to mix ingredients in too small of a bowl. For bulk fermentation (or what many baking books call the first rise), the size is just as much of a factor. During bulk fermentation, the dough doubles, if not triples, in size, so make sure that the bowl has enough volume to accommodate that.

You'll need a large bowl for mixing nine-pound batches of dough like this on a heavy day of baking.

Personally, I prefer stainless steel bowls for mixing and ceramic or glass bowls for bulk fermentation. The stainless steel is light to handle and easy to clean, making it ideal for mixing while the ceramic and glass are thicker and thus more insulating. This allows the bowl to retain more heat during bulk fermentation for a better rise.

Bench Knives and Bowl Scrapers

Bench knives are composed of a metal blade with a wood, metal, or plastic handle. They are used to scrape dough from the bench, or work, surface. They can also be used to slide under the dough to move it from one location to another, for dividing the dough during preshaping, and perfect for shaping certain types of bread, such as *fougasse,* or bread shaped like a leaf.

Before purchasing a bench knife, I suggest you go to a store that has a variety so that you can pick each of them up, mimic some of the actions you'll be using while working with the dough, and decide which one feels best. Pick the one that feels the most natural in your hand; I guarantee that you'll be surprised at how different they feel.

Bowl scrapers, on the other hand, are made from flexible plastic and are used to mix dough and scrape the sides of the bowl (while mixing) to make sure that all ingredients are being incorporated into the dough. Bowl scrapers can also perform the same functions as the bench scraper, although it takes a bit more effort to cut with them; which you use is a personal choice.

Personally, I think it's helpful to have on hand both a small and large bowl scraper. The large is great for mixing while the small is helpful for removing dough from a bowl after bulk fermentation. Its smaller size allows you to be easier on the dough when

it sticks to the sides. What's more, the small, rigid scrapers are a charm for scraping dough from your work surface if you don't want to scratch the surface.

All bowl scrapers are not created equal. Some are much more flexible than others. See which works best for you, but experience has told me that the more flexible the bowl scraper is, the harder it is on your hands. And when you're working with five or more pounds of dough at a time, wear and tear on the hands is definitely a factor to bear in mind.

Bannetons

Bannetons are baskets, which are typically made from cane (although there are plastic ones, too) are what you will use to proof (some books call this the second rise) dough for round or oval (or even triangular) shapes. Some have cloth liners while others are bare cane. No matter which type you use, make sure that they are well floured before placing the dough in them so that the dough doesn't stick. And although they are by no means necessary for the baker, they certainly come in handy for giving dough a head start on maintaining its shape during the proofing process. (Plus they leave a very cool circular pattern on the finished loaf. Use these and people will definitely be

talking about your bread!) However, you can always use a bowl to accomplish the same feat, but I've found that the dough has a tendency to stick more to a bowl, so I opt for the *banneton* any time I can.

Couche, Towels, Plastic Wrap, and Parchment Paper

This category of equipment is used throughout the baking process. The *couche*, towels, and plastic wrap are essential for bulk fermentation and proofing while the parchment paper comes into play during the baking phase of certain types of bread—mainly enriched dough.

A *couche* is a piece of cloth made from linen, typically around a square yard in size, that is used to cover dough during bulk fermentation and proofing so that the dough does not dry out. It is also widely used to help baguettes and ciabatta maintain their form after final shaping and during proofing. You will see how the *couche* is incorporated for these purposes in the techniques and recipes chapter that follow.

How To Season A *Couche*: When you purchase a *couche*, it comes unseasoned. That is, it's just a piece of cloth, and if you were to place it as is on your dough as it rises, the dough would stick to it. Because of this, you have to season it before use. To do so, lay the *couche* out on a table. Sprinkle liberal amounts of flour across the entire surface of the fabric. After that, use your hands to rub the flour into the linen. Within a few strokes of your hands, the *couche* will feel cool and slippery. Once you've worked the flour into the entire *couche*, brush off the excess flour, and it's ready to go. Never, never wash your *couche*. The more you use it and the more you reincorporate flour into it as needed, the better the *couche* will perform for you. And once you start working with it, you'll realize that it's better than plastic wrap.

Many bakers also use smaller linen or cotton towels to cover bowls of dough during bulk fermentation. As with the *couche*, it's advisable to season these as well so that they do not stick to the dough. Trust me, one incident of sticking is enough to drive you to the brink of insanity, so be sure to take the time to see to it that your towels are well floured and as Teflon-like as possible.

In addition to natural cloth, plastic wrap is also a necessity in the bakery. You can use it as a substitute for a *couche* in covering dough during bulk fermentation and proofing. The one major benefit of plastic wrap over *couche*s and towels is that the plastic wrap can be applied to make a container airtight. This is a wonderful benefit if you are baking in an area that is low in humidity as it helps to keep the dough from drying out, or if your kitchen is drafty, which also prevents the dough from drying out. On top of that, one additional benefit—and this is really a big one when you're just starting out—is that you can see through the plastic wrap, which will allow you to better keep track of what your dough is doing during the bulk fermentation and proofing processes.

Lastly, you'll definitely need some parchment paper, which you can purchase at most grocery stores. Parchment paper is a specially processed type of paper that is used to line baking pans and sheets so that the dough will not stick to the metallic surface during baking. Essentially, it's a substitute for greasing a pan. However,

when it comes right down to it, I still prefer to grease a pan over using parchment paper. It just seems more authentic to me. And you'll also find that sometimes that greasing a pan and then spreading some

Although parchment paper can be used in place of wax paper, the opposite is not true as wax paper will smoke in a hot oven. And that's the last thing you want in your home bakery.

cornmeal over the greased area works just as well as the parchment.

Lame or Knife

Here, you're introduced to yet another French term: *lame*, which is the device used to score or slash the surface of the dough before baking. The idea behind scoring dough is twofold: one, it allows for maximum expansion of the bread during the baking process, and two, its form serves as the baker's signature, her mark of artistic creativity on the finished bread.

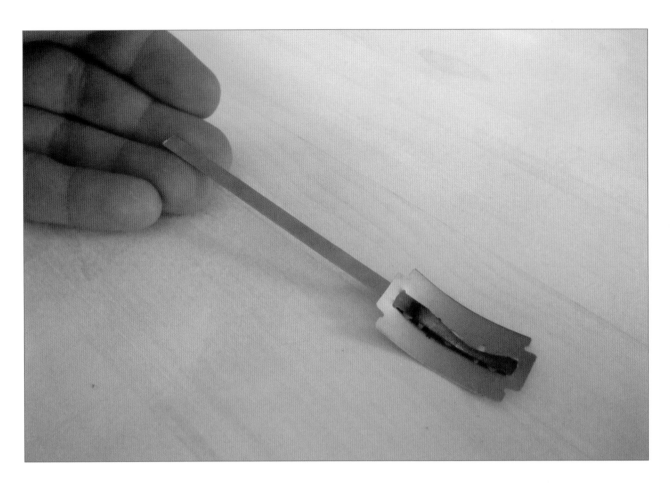

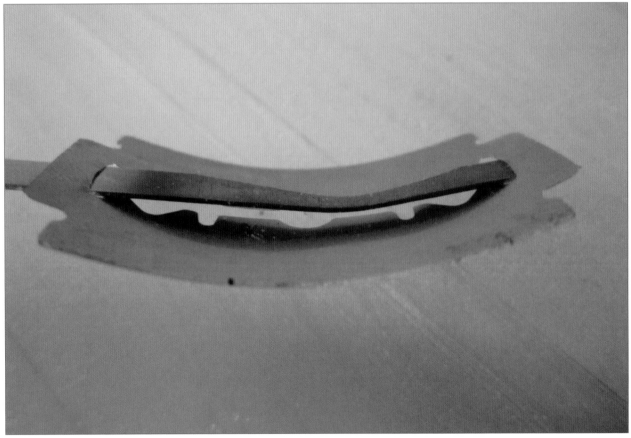

HOW TO MAKE YOUR OWN *LAME*:

1. Purchase a double-edged razor, which can be obtained at most drug stores, and a coffee stir stick, which can be obtained at most grocery stores.

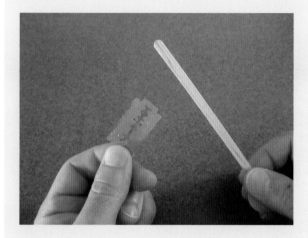

2. Insert the stir stick into one of the end holes on the razor.

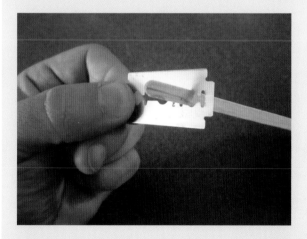

3. Push the stick toward the other end of the razor and thread it through the end hole at the other end.

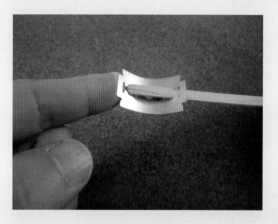

4. Your *lame* is now ready for use.

You may prefer to use only a razor and not a *lame*. Using the razor alone allows you to cut to different depths in the dough more easily, and because the distance between the dough and your hand is less, you will have more control over your scoring.

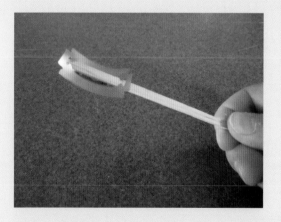

Note: If you find that your *lame* is sticking or dragging when you're working with very wet dough, try applying a thin coat of oil to the blade. It will help the blade move more easily through the dough.

If you don't have a *lame* or don't want to make or use one, you can always use a knife. Just make sure that the knife is extremely sharp, as a dull blade will prevent a smooth, even cut. Also, use a straight-edged knife because with a serrated edge, it's much easier for the knife to snag on the dough, thus creating an improper slice on the dough's surface.

Thermometers

Thermometers are one type of equipment that just never seem to be addressed with much detail. To me, thermometers rank second only to the scale in importance. Why? Because temperature is so important throughout the entire bread-baking process and is critical to overall success.

A good pair of kitchen shears is necessary for properly shaping *épi de blé*.

Specifically, there are three areas where thermometers come into play: ambient air (room) temperature, dough temperature, and oven temperature. The ambient air temperature will not only determine the rate at which dough rises during bulk fermentation and proofing (if you're not using your oven to do so), but it will also impact the internal temperature of the dough, which must exist at a precise level to create an optimal environment for the dough to develop. And the oven temperature is critical for creating a nice crust as well as making sure that the crumb is fully baked.

To meet the bread baker's needs, two types of thermometers are necessary. The first is the chef's thermometer and the second is the oven thermometer. The chef's thermometer can be used to determine ambient air temperature, internal dough temperature, temperature during bulk fermentation and proofing, and baked bread temperature, signifying when it's ready to come out of the oven. The oven thermometer is absolutely essential for assessing the actual temperature of your oven. You'd be surprised at how "off" your oven might be from the temperature your oven tells you it's at. And if your oven is not accurate, you can be almost certain that your bread will reflect that.

But simply having the right kind of thermometers is not enough. In order for them to aid you, rather than cause you more problems, your thermometers must be calibrated so that the temperature you read on their dials is the actual temperature of whatever you are measuring.

Here's how to calibrate your chef's thermometer:

1. Fill a container half full with water and half full with ice and wait several minutes for the water to chill.

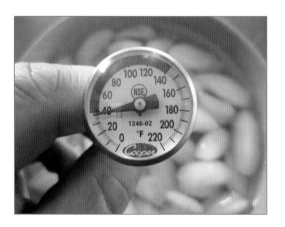

2. Insert the shaft of the thermometer into the ice water bath. Do not allow the tip of thermometer to touch the bottom or sides of the bowl. Keep it suspended in the center. The thermometer should read 32°F. If it does, your thermometer is properly calibrated. If it does not, your thermometer must be calibrated.

3. Turn the thermometer upside down to locate the nut directly underneath the dial.

4. Firmly hold the nut with the pliers.

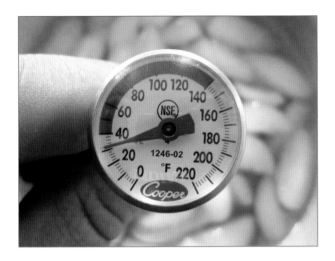

5. Rotate the dial clockwise or counterclockwise until the hand on the dial points to 32°F. (The dial can be a bit stiff to turn, so put a little bit of muscle into it if you need to.) Your thermometer is now calibrated.

You can make sure that your oven thermometer is calibrated correctly by immersing it in a bowl of boiling water to see if the temperature reads near 212°F. However, in order to do this, the thermometer must be waterproof, and unfortunately, these are tough to find.

If you're using digital thermometers, refer to your manufacturer for instructions on how to calibrate their devices.

Baking Sheets and Pans

This category of equipment is similar to bowl scrapers: all baking sheets and pans are not created equal. This is not merely a cost issue for some highly priced sheets and pans can wreak more havoc than the least expensive. But as a general rule, the pans that perform the best are those that are thicker and darker. The thickness of the pan allows for even retention and distribution of heat while the darker color allows the dough to brown properly. A lighter pan just won't allow the dough to get to that golden stage of color development. Ultimately, you're going to have to experiment to find out what works best for you and your oven, but these guidelines will help you arrive at the right product faster. And when you find a pan or sheet that works for you and your oven, then stick with it.

As for what kinds of pans you'll need, I suggest three: a sheet pan, a loaf pan, and a Pullman pan if you can afford it. In the absence of a baking stone, the sheet pan will serve you well for baguettes, *batards*, *boules*, and other non-pan-shaped loaves of bread. It will also help prevent burning the bottom of enriched dough like challah or brioche. The loaf pan is essential for many types of enriched dough, like brioche. And the Pullman pan, which is a loaf pan with a sliding lid, is perfect for creating *pain de mie*, the French, and quite frankly superior

Pullman, sheet, and loaf pans

by anyone's standards, version of American-style white bread.

The Baker's Peel and Flipping Board

In a commercial bakery, bakers use what's called a peel to move their dough into the oven. It's a wide, thin sheet of wood or metal with a handle. The dough is placed on them and then slid into the depths of the commercial oven. If you haven't seen them at work in a bakery, you've most likely seen them used at a pizza place. Although they are great to have around and use, the main problem for the home baker is that they can be too large and cumbersome to use within the confines of the home kitchen. However, there are some suppliers who offer twelve-by-twelve-inch versions that are small enough to handle in the home. But if purchasing a baker's peel is not an option for you, then a simple alternative is the back of a baking sheet or, better yet, a good old-fashioned piece of stiff cardboard. You can cut it to whatever size you'd like, but ten inches by twenty-four inches is a

Peel with *batard* on it.

great all-around size. It will allow you to slide large *boules*, or round-shaped loaves, into your oven as well as twenty-inch long baguettes (and we all know that longer is better than shorter when it comes to baguettes!). Plus it's economical, won't clutter up your kitchen, and is easily replaceable. Just make sure you cut it neatly so cardboard won't end up in your dough.

For all practical purposes, a flipping board is a long, narrow peel without a handle. It's used with baguettes to transfer them from the *couche* upon which they've proofed to the oven without damaging the integrity of the dough. But, as with the peel,

Flipping board with baguette on it.

if you don't have a flipping board, make one out of cardboard. It will do the trick just fine. You'll learn how to use it in the baking section of the book.

Pastry Brushes

Although you can certainly make do without these, pastry brushes can help to make a job easier. Their use in bread baking is limited to brushing liquid—usually eggs, egg whites, or milk—on the surface of the dough before baking. Doing so can help in two ways: first, it can help to create a crunchy crust, which is particularly true of

egg whites, and second, it is a great way to create a perfectly golden crust, both of which add greatly to the quality of the final product.

Be aware that pastry brushes can be soft or stiff, and the only way to really tell is to feel them. I highly recommend the use of a soft-bristled brush. It will allow you to apply the ingredient—eggs, milk, etc.,—without damaging the surface of the dough. Stiffer bristles may dent the dough, thus damaging the structure of the dough, which is something you want to avoid at all costs. Also, because the softer bristles are much more flexible, they allow you to coat the

tough-to-reach areas of the dough's surface much more easily. This is most often helpful with braided dough, such as challah, and other uniquely shaped dough.

Spray Bottle

A good old-fashioned spray bottle works wonders for creating steam in the oven during the baking process, which is highly beneficial for producing that artisan-style crust we all love. Just remember that when you use it, fill it with purified water if possible since that water will necessarily be coming into contact with your dough. I'll provide you with further instructions on how and when to use it in the section on baking.

Baking Stone

In ranking the value of equipment, the baking stone is a very close second to the scale in terms of impact on the finished product—at least for the home baker. Baking stones help to make your home oven work more like a professional oven. In fact, they go even one step further: they help to transform your oven into an old-school brick oven just like you'd find in some parts of France or Italy.

Baking stones are made of clay—although some are engineered composite material—and are placed in the oven before you begin to heat your oven for baking. The stone heats up to the same temperature as the oven so that when you put your dough directly on it, as you do for many artisan-

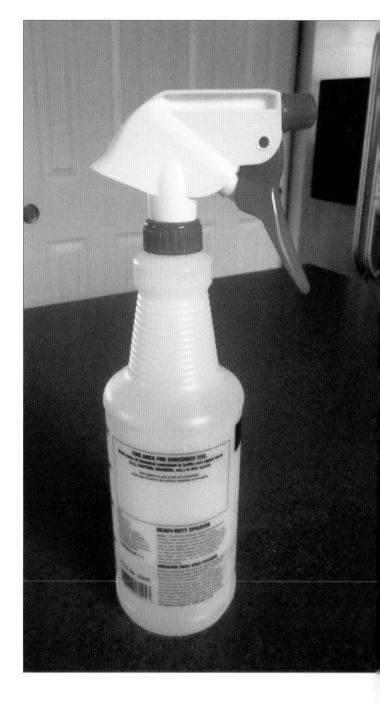

style breads, the dough is baking from the first second it's placed on the stone. This creates a nicely browned and crispy bottom on the bread. And because they retain heat well, they aid in keeping the oven at the desired temperature throughout the baking process. This is important in those instances when you have to open the oven door several times to add moisture during the baking process.

The main factor in choosing a baking stone is thickness: the thicker the stone, the better. If possible, purchase one in the ¾ inch to one-inch thickness range. The thicker stone will retain and transfer heat more readily than the thinner versions. Plus, the thinner stones are more likely to crack at an earlier stage in their baking careers. See the reference guide for a place to purchase these.

Comparison of thick versus thin baking stone.

No matter what, avoid putting water directly on a hot stone. It greatly increases the chances of the stone cracking, warping, or at a minimum, prematurely aging.

Cooling Racks

Last, but certainly not least, we come to cooling racks. I cannot tell you how disappointed you will be if you spend all those hours baking your first loaf of bread but don't cool it properly. You'll cut into it, hoping to experience nirvana, but instead, you'll find a gluey inside that just doesn't rise to your level of expectations in the taste category. If you don't believe me, cut into your next loaf right out of the oven and then cut into in several hours later, and you'll understand what I'm saying. The flavor that comes through once bread has been properly cooled speaks for itself.

To cool the bread, you'll need some type of cooling racks. There's really nothing complicated about them. The idea is to keep the loaf of bread off a solid surface so

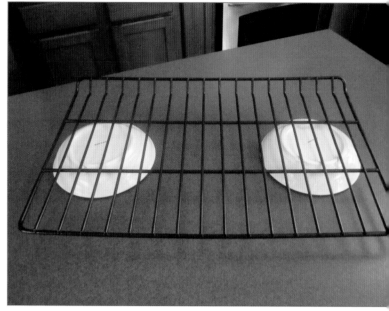

Improvised cooling rack.

that air can circulate around it, thus cooling it. In commercial bakeries, there are racks specifically designed for this purpose; however, sometimes you'll even see bakers take their bread right from the oven and place it on stainless steel storage racks with wire shelves. That does the trick just fine.

You can do the same at home with a relatively inexpensive cooling rack that you can purchase at virtually every cooking and baking supply store, not to mention most of your large department stores and chain megastores. But if you don't have one, and you want to start baking right away and don't want to run out and buy one, you can take one of the extra racks out of your oven and elevate it off your work area by placing it on an upside-down plate at each end (or anything really that will keep the rack from resting directly on the work surface). It

works just the same in a pinch, and you don't need to clutter up your cabinets with yet another piece of equipment right off the bat. But when you do get the chance, purchase a cooling rack. It makes life in the home bakery that much easier.

In your career as a baker, there's no doubt that you'll come across a multitude of other ingredients and pieces of equipment. Some of them will come in quite handy in the home bakery while others will cause you nothing but grief. I strongly suggest that before you begin experimenting, you must master the use and incorporation of the ingredients and tools I discussed above. Not only will they arm you with the knowledge to bake a wide variety of bread, but you will develop a sixth-sense for calculating the usefulness of every other ingredient and piece of equipment out there.

Techniques

IT COMES DOWN TO THIS: WITHOUT PROPER technique, it doesn't matter how wonderful your flour is or that you'll be baking your bread in a $40,000 deck oven. The result will be the same—a less than perfect loaf of bread. Furthermore, when you consider the fact that creating flavorful breads requires a time investment of anywhere from several hours to more than a day, it makes getting your technique right on the first try all the more important. I for one can vouch for the fact that it is not a feel-good moment when you spend a day developing a preferment, then several hours perfecting the dough, only to find out in the eleventh hour that you forgot to properly steam the oven prior to baking. And instead of finding a crispy crust on your bread, you discover a crust as crunchy as cotton balls.

Ultimately, this chapter will serve as the foundation upon which the remainder of the book is based. Devoting the time and effort to understanding and implementing these techniques will help to solidify your chances of creating a sought-after product from your first attempt forward.

It is important to note, however, that a discussion of technique necessarily requires plentiful reference to the ingredients and equipment that were detailed in the previous chapter. At any time you do not recall what an ingredient or article of equipment is or where it fits into the grand scheme of the technique I am explaining, I encourage you to revisit that portion of the book, reread it, and then return to where you previously left off.

At this stage of your education into the essentials of break baking, I need to tell you something: baking delicious, picture-perfect bread is not easy. It takes passion, effort, and determination, and without this book, it unfortunately can take a lot of errors. But—and this is a big *but*—if you have the aptitude and are willing to devote just a little bit of time, you will be able to conquer the craft of bread baking in no time at all. In the same breath, you'll discover that bread baking provides you with little rewards and encouragement all along the way: you can see your dough turn into "rags" as you're mixing (telling you you're doing it right), you'll watch your dough puff up like a proud peacock during bulk fermentation (meaning that you're right on track), and you'll smile as your dough splits open under the swift gash of your *lame* (signifying that you proofed it to the perfect degree). It is these small, but oh-so-fulfilling rewards that you'll soon discover for yourself that will cause you to keep reading, studying, and pursuing the perfect loaf of bread—from conception to completion.

That said, go wash your hands. It's time to get dirty.

The Eight Essential Steps of Bread Baking

Baking bread is, first and foremost, logical. It is the result of well-reasoned thinking and strict adherence to that line of thinking throughout the baking process. In reality, this presents a win-win situation for the baker. First, the baker does not have to invent her own logic to create bakery-quality bread since it's already been worked out and tested over the past several thousand years. And second, following the already established logic of bread making necessarily infers that a logical result will arise, which, of course, is nothing less than a delicious and beautiful loaf of bread.

Fortunately for all of us with the desire to bake bread, the logic of bread baking is contained within a series of steps that layout the entire process. They are the following:

1. Preparing the *mise en place*—gathering together all the equipment and ingredients required for the recipe.

2. Mixing ingredients—preparing and adding ingredients in the proper order and using the proper technique to ensure that all ingredients unite to form dough.

3. Kneading—distributing ingredients evenly throughout the dough and properly developing the structure of the dough.

4. Bulk fermentation—creating an environment to encourage the development of structure and flavor within the dough.

5. Preshaping—forming the dough into a preliminary shape to help strengthen the structure of the dough.

6. Final shaping—manipulating the dough into the form at which it will be baked.

7. Proofing—allowing the structure of the dough to maximize before baking.

8. Baking and Cooling—preparing the oven and dough for baking and creating an optimal environment for the ultimate taste experience.

Although there are many steps contained within each of these major categories, all are easy to comprehend and even easier to carry out with nothing more than a pinch of patience, a cup of effort, and a fifty-pound sack of desire.

> Always take meticulous notes throughout all of your baking endeavors, particularly when you're just starting out. It will help you to troubleshoot down the road.

Step One: Preparing Your *Mise en Place*

Mise en place is a French term and means, quite simply, "set in place." Its application to baking—and all of life for that matter—is basic: get all your ingredients together and equipment lined up before beginning. This allows you to make sure that you are fully prepared to tackle a recipe without having to backtrack or look for some tool or whatever else you might when time is least on your side.

Bear in mind, your *mise en place* does not just refer to getting your ingredients and equipment in order. No, it means getting your mind in order as well. In fact, it could be argued, quite successfully, that

organizing your thoughts is much more important than gathering your ingredients and equipment, for you can never gather the latter unless you first gather the former.

So, what does this mean? Well, the first part of putting your mind in the right place is to consider the end game—just what are you trying to accomplish? Your goal—I hope—is to bake the perfect loaf of bread. That begs the question: What kind of loaf are you baking? Knowing the answer to this question will help you to plan what recipe to use, what the final shape of the loaf will be, how to score the loaf, if at all, and how much steam to create in the oven, to name a few considerations.

Once you've determined what recipe you're using and what you want the bread to look like when you remove it from the oven, then you can backtrack to gather the items you need to make that happen. Although I can provide you with certain guidance on what you should be thinking about as you being your journey into the wonderful world of bread baking, you'll soon hone in on your own list of things you need to gather that are dependent upon your time frame, your kitchen, your ingredients, and most important, your taste.

Certain things to bear in mind once you decide to bake a loaf a bread include how long it takes your oven to preheat, how long you'll need to bake the bread, what the ambient air temperature and humidity levels are in your kitchen, how long it will take you to mix and knead your dough, how long you'll need to rest your dough after

An important but often overlooked aspect of the *mise en place* is considering what's beneath your feet. Since you're going to be doing a lot of standing during the baking process, make sure that you're wearing comfortable shoes or, better yet, put some padding underneath your feet while working. It will go a long way toward preventing back problems and fatigue.

preshaping, and more. This is a perfect situation to get out that notebook and start planning your attack. There's no doubt you'll have a lot going on in the pages to come, so a few well-chosen notes will help you remember those details that you just won't want to forget.

But aside from mentally preparing, you'll need to prepare your ingredients and equipment as well. The equipment we'll use is minimal, and you'll learn in rapid fashion just what you need as you advance through the rest of the techniques section and the recipes section. Preparing the ingredients, however, requires a bit more explanation because it will most definitely impact the quality of the final product.

For all practical purposes, your main focus must be on scaling or weighing out your ingredients. And by weighing out your ingredients, I mean weighing all of them *before* you do anything else. This way you will have everything you need at your disposal at the precise moment when you need it.

> Remember to use the tare weight function on your scale so you're only measuring the weight of the ingredient and not the container.

> Add ingredients slowly during the weighing process. That way you won't have to waste time removing ingredients because you poured too much into the container in the first place.

After you've weighed all your ingredients, assemble all the bowls, scrapers, towels, *couches*, *lames*, and other items you will need throughout the rest of the baking process. This way you won't have to search around looking for an item and accidentally miss a step or lose your train of thought.

You will realize in very short order that compiling your mind-set, ingredients, and equipment before you do anything else will set the tone for moving through the remainder of the steps with ease and enjoyment. This is the way professional bakers do it, so why not start acting like a professional from the beginning?

Step Two: Mixing Ingredients

Mixing ingredients is as critical to the quality of the final product as any other portion of the process. If this strikes you as a surprise, I encourage you to take just a moment to consider this scenario: What if you took a bite of your favorite bread and all you tasted was salt? It's definitely not what you expected, and even if you are a salt-lover like me, I seriously doubt that it would entice anyone to sink her teeth into the crust again. Although this may be an extreme example, it does illustrate the importance of properly combining and mixing ingredients. But even more significant, the ingredients must work in harmony in order to produce a high-quality product, and mixing them in the right manner will help to make this a reality.

As you learned in the previous chapter, each of the ingredients plays a particular role in the creation of dough. Although it may seem that you can simply dump all of the ingredients in a bowl, stir, and start kneading, the truth is that adding certain ingredients at the wrong time can set you up for failure (meaning a less than perfect loaf of bread)—even though it may take another one to three hours to realize it. It's bad enough to know you made a mistake and see failure instantaneously but another thing completely when you have invested a lot more time and effort only to experience the same result. Hopefully by now, you

A large part of achieving success in mixing is doing so by hand. Yes, it is certainly possible to mix ingredients using a commercial mixer. High-volume bakeries have no choice but to use them, and some people have to use them at home for various reasons. But, I'd bet that if you ask any baker worth her flour, she'd tell you that there's just something about mixing ingredients by hand that creates a better product. Maybe none can state with 100 percent certainty just why that's so, but sometimes faith in the unquantifiable really is the answer, and with bread, this may never ring more true. Plus, there are a few perks to hand mixing, such as not having to lug out the big table top mixer and less to clean up afterward. And, if you're anything like me, the latter is all the justification needed.

Three Types of Dough: Straight Dough in which all ingredients are mixed together at one time, Prefermented Dough in which yeast, flour, and water are combined to varying degrees and allowed to ferment (several hours to several days) prior to mixing with the rest of the ingredients, and Enriched Dough in which sugar and/or fat are included in a recipe.

understand that the importance of this step cannot be overstated.

The upside to all of this is that combining and mixing ingredients is such a basic process that there's absolutely no reason or excuse whatsoever for being careless and leaving it to chance. All you have to do is follow the instructions in the proper order, and you'll be guaranteed success.

BEFORE YOU BEGIN MIXING:

1. Wash your hands (and rewash them throughout the baking process as needed). I'm always perplexed that so many cookbooks never mention this basic premise of cleanliness. It is critical to preventing the introduction of germs and bacteria into the bread—or any other food for that matter.
2. Make sure that all your tools *and* your work surface are clean before you begin. It's essential to health, and it makes working all that much easier. This is how the professionals do it, so if you want to create the same result, don't skimp here.

Here's how it's done:

1. Place your ingredients within easy reach of your mixing area.
2. Add the yeast to the flour.
3. Use a whisk to blend together the flour and yeast. Doing so will help to ensure that the yeast is properly distributed throughout the dough.
4. Add the salt and mix it into the flour and yeast mixture.

5. Pour the water into the bowl. (Make sure it's the right temperature! I'll discuss this in detail below.)

6. Hold the dough scraper in your dominant hand and hold onto the rim of the bowl with your nondominant hand.

7. Slide the dough scraper down the inside of the bowl, between the bowl and the ingredients. Slide the dough scraper underneath the ingredients and toward the center of the bowl, lifting the dough scraper up and toward the opposite side of the bowl, turning your hand over and making sure to carry along a scraper full of ingredients. With your nondominant hand, rotate the bowl in the direction of the hand holding the scraper.

8. Repeat steps 6 and 7, all the while scraping down the sides of the bowl to make sure that all of the ingredients are mixed in. When the ingredients begin to combine, stir them together until they look like "rags." (Enriched dough will be much more firm, having the appearance of stiff cookie dough. Dough with a higher hydration [water content] level, such as *ciabatta*, will look looser, like it can barely hold itself together.)

9. At this point, use the bowl scraper or your hand to begin folding the dough upon itself until it forms a rough ball.

10. When a rough ball has formed, slide the dough out of the bowl and onto your work surface. The dough is now ready for kneading.

When mixing a prefermented dough (discussed later on), mix the water, preferment, and salt (and sugar and fat if required) first then add the flour and yeast. After that, proceed with mixing just as described above.

When mixing an enriched dough (discussed later on) that incorporates large amounts of butter, mix all the ingredients together first then mix in the butter.

MIXING TIPS

- Always keep one hand clean while mixing. It allows you to grab a towel or move items from your work area without contaminating them with dough—and making a mess.
- If the ingredients stick to your dough scraper and won't let go, use the straight edge of a butter knife (or another scraper) to scrape the dough scraper clean, adding the scraped-off ingredients back into the bowl where they belong.
- If you have the choice, it's always better to use a larger rather than smaller bowl for mixing. A larger bowl gives you plenty of room to move the ingredients around without having to worry about the ingredients cascading over the edge. This way you can concentrate on

technique rather than worrying about losing those valuable components of your recipe.

- When you are beginning your journey into bread baking, it always appears that the recipe called for way too much flour when you place it in the bowl, and at the end, it inevitably appears that the recipe called for too much water and is much wetter than you'd think. Don't worry, when the mixing techniques demonstrated here are combined with the kneading techniques described shortly, the dough will come together as needed. Practical translation: never, never add flour or water beyond what the recipe calls for just because the dough looks too dry or too wet in the beginning.

- Don't let anyone or any equipment manufacturer fool you; the best mixing devices in existence are your hands, so don't be afraid to use them. Feel free to be a kid again and get your hands dirty. Sometimes that's the only way to get the dough to come together. (If you don't believe me, skip ahead to the recipe on brioche, where I show you the messiness of incorporating butter into the dough.) Plus, as you'll soon read about in the kneading section, the warmth from your hands can help the dough to attain, or at least maintain, its optimal internal temperature, which is critical for the success of the remainder of the baking operation.

- Be sure to scrape all the ingredients out of their original bowls when combining ingredients, and be sure to scrape all the dough out of the mixing container when you scrape it onto the work surface for kneading. Doing so will help to ensure that all the original proportions of ingredients remain intact throughout the mixing process. This is critical for very wet dough, like *ciabatta* and some sourdough, which is extremely sticky and will remain in the bowl if you're not diligent about getting it out.

As you will soon read, the temperature of the dough is very important. So when you mix your ingredients, make sure you are using a bowl that is room temperature. If it's not, heat it in the microwave for short bursts of time (if it's microwave-safe) to warm it, or if it's heat-proof, move it back and forth over a burner on the stove to warm it up. You'll realize how helpful this will be in just a few paragraphs.

Step Three: Kneading

Kneading is one of those activities that looks really simple when someone else is doing it—particularly someone with a great deal of experience—and then when you try it for the first time, you come to the undesirable conclusion that you are much more awkward than you would have thought. But rest assured this is one event where persistence, patience, and repetition pay off.

I am going to cover two different techniques for kneading, although one of them isn't so much kneading in the conventional sense as it is working the dough in a special way to achieve the same result as conventional kneading. I want to let you know before we begin that you're going to have a much easier time getting the hang of conventional kneading, or the type that most of us picture in our minds from watching our grandmothers or bakers on television, than you are with the second type of kneading, which is a French technique that is a bit trickier to master. But if you'll just allow yourself to let loose during the process of working through the French technique, it will be a much easier ride— and it's pretty fun once you get the hang of it. That said, neither is difficult, nor do either require an advanced degree to accomplish. It's just like with many new things we learn in life; some are easier than others.

> Although kneading is open to broad interpretation, the methods I describe here are the two most prevalent, and they also happen to be the most effective for dealing with almost any dough.

> Taste the dough after you knead it. It will give you a good idea if the dough will be flavorful—particularly the salt component—after it's baked.

The question then becomes twofold: What is kneading, and what does it do for the dough?

Kneading is the process of working the dough with your hands—or a mixer if necessary—in a particular way after the ingredients have been mixed. Proper kneading is essential to being able to advance through the rest of the steps in the baking process. Without it, bulk fermentation, shaping, proofing, and baking will never work the way they should, and ultimately, you'll end up with a dense shape of something that nowhere resembles what you imagined your bread to look like when you began your endeavor.

Kneading achieves several different things in the bread-baking process. First, it helps to mix the ingredients so that they are uniformly distributed in the dough. Second, the warmth of your hands—along with the warmth of the ingredients, equipment, and room—help to activate the yeast. And third, and arguably the most important, kneading aids in gluten development in the dough.

Let's focus on this last benefit—gluten development—for a moment. As I covered in the flour discussion in section 1, gluten plays a key role in the development of what will eventually become bread. The higher gluten content of bread flour provides the building blocks for creating a framework within the dough so that a high-quality loaf of bread will come out of the oven in the end. During the kneading process, the gluten elongates to create structure within the dough that will cause gas to become trapped within the dough during the fermentation and proofing processes. This structure is what allows the dough to rise, for without it, the dough would remain flat and never achieve its potential.

This brings us back to how we will achieve this. We'll use one of the two techniques or a combination of the two. Conventional kneading seems to work best for dough that has a lower hydration level. The hydration level is the percentage of water (or other liquid) in the dough when compared to the amount of flour. For example, if a recipe calls for 1,000 grams of flour and 650 grams of water, the hydration level is 65 percent (or 650 divided by 1,000). The key to arriving at the correct hydration level is that both the water and the flour must be expressed in the same unit of measurement—weight. All too often recipes call for flour in grams or ounces and water in milliliters or fluid ounces. By using the weight of both the flour and water, you'll be making an apples-to-apples comparison, and calculate the right hydration level.

For the most part, you find that most recipes fit neatly into two categories of hydration level: those consisting of approximately 65 percent–68 percent and those consisting of greater than 68 percent. The former is more suited for conventional kneading, while the latter is better for the French style of kneading. However, I have found that certain dough responds best to a combination of both. So let's take a look at how you perform both.

CONVENTIONAL METHOD

1. On an unfloured work surface, place the ball of dough directly in front of you with the heel of your hand on top of the dough.

2. With the heel of your hand, push the dough downward (toward the work surface) and forward with a smooth stroke. Make sure that you are pushing hard enough that the dough moves underneath your hand, but not so hard that the dough begins to tear. When you have pushed the dough so that the heel of your hand is at the front edge of the

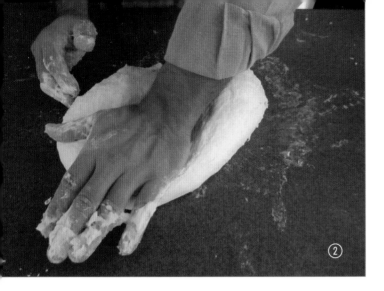

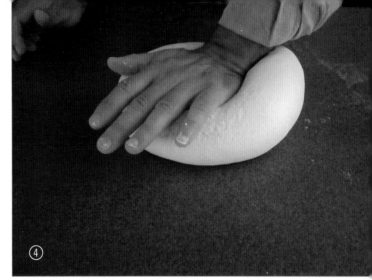

dough, remove your hand from the dough.

3. With your other hand, fold the dough in half, and move the dough back to where it started before the first knead.

4. Repeat steps 1 through 4 until the dough becomes smooth and the gluten has been developed to the desired degree.

There are as many variations on how to knead dough as there are bakers, so find what works best for you and go with it—so long as the gluten becomes properly developed.

CONVENTIONAL KNEADING TIPS

- Work the dough as close to your body as possible to alleviate unnecessary pressure on your back.
- Focus on pushing the dough, not rolling it or compressing it.
- Resist the urge to add flour to the dough. The more you knead, the more air will be incorporated into the dough and the more the flour will absorb the water. Both will help to combat what appears to be excessive moisture.
- If the dough sticks to your work surface, use the stiff bowl scraper (or bench knife

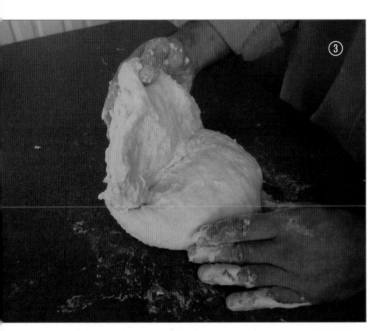

if it won't scratch your surface by doing so) to scrape the bits of dough from the surface and return them to the rest of the dough.

- If you find that you are getting tired during the process, switch hands. It might take a little getting used to as far as coordination goes, but once you get the hang of it, you'll be able to work through the kneading process that much easier.
- As you knead the dough, you will notice that it transforms into something much smoother and more elastic. This means that the dough is developing precisely the way you want it to. So keep doing what you're doing.
- If you use the conventional method to knead dough with a greater hydration level, it is helpful to use the bowl scraper instead of your hand to gather the dough and fold it upon itself during the kneading process. If you use your hands, the dough sometimes sticks to them so much that it's hard to keep the dough together.

- If you decide to make larger batches of dough, be aware that the heavier weight of the dough takes more effort on your part. Keep that in mind so you don't wear yourself out before the dough makes it to the oven!

FRENCH METHOD

This French method was most likely originally seen by American viewers decades ago on Julia Child's *The French Chef*. In more recent times, it has been popularized by the highly talented Richard Bertinet in his book, *Dough*. And there are some great videos on the internet from different bakers, showing their takes on this timeless technique.

1. After using the bowl scraper to remove the wetter dough from the mixing bowl, place the dough directly in front of you.

2. Placing your hands under the top edge of the dough, gather it together.

3. Lift the dough off the work surface.

4. Continue lifting the dough until it is about chest high. The palms of your hands should be facing your body.

5. When you stop lifting the dough upward, rotate your hands so that your palms are facing down. The dough will be flipped over the back of your hands at this point.

6. Move the dough downward toward the work surface, accelerating as your hands descend. As your hands are moving downward, the dough will stretch. The dough should "slap" against the work surface.

7. When the dough comes into contact with the work surface, rotate your hands toward you (leading with your little finger; your palms will rotate until they are facing you), and slightly lift that end of the elongated dough up.

8. Bring your hands forward, stretch the dough outward to the sides, and fold the dough upon itself.

9. Gather the dough together as you did in step 2; repeat steps 3 through 9.

10. After repeating this process fifteen to twenty times, the dough will begin to come together. Continue kneading until the gluten has developed to the required degree.

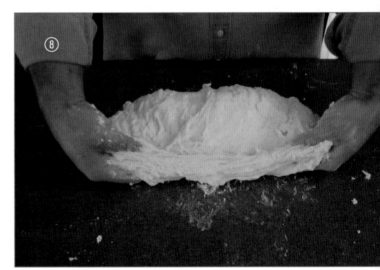

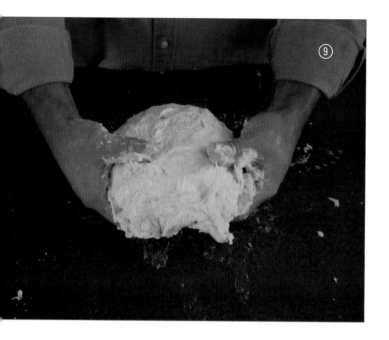

One of the main benefits of the French method is that it stretches the dough and incorporates air into the dough. These two factors heavily contribute to getting a very wet dough to come together so that you can work with it during the shaping, proofing, and baking stages.

This technique does not work very well with dough below 68 percent hydration or with enriched dough. For those, use the conventional method; it will make your work much easier.

FRENCH KNEADING TIPS

- The dough is going to feel too wet to work with. Don't worry; after a dozen or so kneads, the dough will begin to come together better. This is a result of the air that is incorporated into the dough every time it stretches and then is folded upon itself.
- Although it seems like the dough is never going to come off of your hands, it will. As the dough develops, it will eventually be incorporated into the rest of the dough.
- If you feel uncoordinated and out of control at first, welcome to the club. This technique is much more difficult to become comfortable with than conventional kneading. And, certainly in the beginning, awkwardness is the name of the game, so this is one technique where practice does make perfect.
- Make sure that you accelerate the dough on the downward movement. This causes the dough to stretch, which develops gluten and incorporates air to allow the dough to achieve its final, workable form.

- A steady rhythm is key with the French method—much more than with conventional kneading. Too slow and the dough will never stretch and develop. Too much speed and the dough will tear. Trial and error is, unfortunately, the only way to master this technique.

- During the early stages of this kneading process, a decent amount of dough may stick to your work surface. Use your bowl scraper or bench knife to scrape it off the surface and add it back to the rest of the dough.

- If this techniques seems violent to you, that's because it is. But somewhere deep within that violence is a magnificent way to knead wetter than average dough. Plus, you can work away some stress while you're doing it—a win-win situation for you and the dough!

- Don't be surprised if you find bits of dough scattered about after your first few attempts at trying this technique. It's bound to happen. (About a week after using this technique on one occasion, I noticed a chunk of dough on the wall, overhead, and behind me a few feet. Man, is it tough to get off the wall after it dries! To avoid scraping dried dough off your walls, I'd recommend taking a look around the area when you first start using this method so that you don't come face-to-face the same scenario I did.)

TEMPERATURE AND TIME

There are two other issues that we must address at this point that will definitely impact the rest of the steps in the process as well as the final product: temperature and time.

Temperature is a key component to successful bread baking—from gathering your *mise en place* to cooling and storing your loaf. It is both the easiest and most difficult component to control. It is easy because you have a large amount of control over the temperature of your ingredients. It is difficult because you cannot control the outside temperature, and you can only partially control the inside temperature of our baking areas. However, it is possible to gain a sufficient amount of control over temperature.

When a baker speaks about temperature, she most often refers to something the pros call "desired dough temperature" or DDT. This is the internal temperature of the dough. The DDT for yeast dough can range between 65°F and 85°F, but most typically falls within the 75°F–80°F range. The DDT is directly impacted by that which I mentioned in the previous paragraph, and its level wholly impacts the remainder of the bread-baking process. The reason for this is that in order for the yeast to develop to the proper extent within the dough—the proper extent being determined by the particular type of bread a baker wants to produce—an optimal environment must be created for it to do so. The only way to do that is to control ambient air temperature and the temperature of the ingredients.

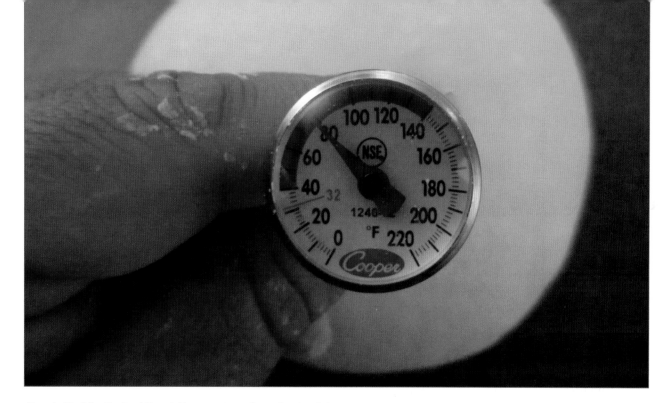

How to Test for Desired Dough Temperature: Once the dough begins to come together into more of what you expect the dough to look like, insert a chef's thermometer into the center of the dough and leave it there for about 30 seconds. Then read the dial, which will provide you with the dough temperature.

Mathematically calculating DDT is complex because of so many variables, including ambient air temperature, temperature of the ingredients, and what's called the "friction factor," or the amount of heat generated during the mixing and kneading processes. You can easily become obsessive-compulsive about this—and it pays in terms of consistency for commercial bakeries—but for the home baker, you'll find that manipulating the water temperature (which will be discussed further below) is the easiest way to get your dough to the right temperature.

Ideally, ambient air temperature should be around 75°F. However, this may not be practical to maintain in the climate in which you live just for the purpose of baking bread, so you have to be flexible. But once the ambient air temperature approaches 60°F on the low end and 80°F on the high end, greater manipulation of the ingredients will be required to offset the ambient air temperature so that the dough can develop at the appropriate DDT.

Although the temperatures of ingredients like flour, yeast, and salt do play a role in achieving the DDT, they take quite a bit of finessing to control. On the other hand, water temperature is much easier to manipulate—i.e., you can easily heat it on the stove to bring it up in temperature or place it in the refrigerator or freezer to lower the temperature. Generally speaking, the warmer the ambient air temperature, the cooler the water that will be used in a recipe and vice versa.

In order to attain the proper DDT in most scenarios, through manipulation of the water temperature, your water temperature will most likely be between 65°F and 100°F. Again, the warmer the ambient air temperature, the cooler the water that can be used. So if your ambient air temperature is hovering near 60°F, use water that is closer to 90°F–100°F. And if the ambient air temperature is in the 80s, then use water that is around 70°F–75°F. Without diving into complex mathematical equations, it's difficult to be completely precise with prescribing a water temperature, but I assure you that after baking a few loaves, you'll quickly get an idea for how warm or cool your water should be.

However, in addition to the ambient air temperature and the temperature of the ingredients, there are two other variables at play in achieving the DDT. The first is friction—which I mentioned earlier—and the second is the temperature of your work surface. Friction plays a role in the DDT because as you knead the dough, you create friction, and the friction produces heat. So the type of kneading and the duration of the kneading will affect the DDT. Practically speaking, conventional kneading will produce much greater heat than the French technique because of the greater contact between the hands and the dough

and the work surface. Duration of kneading will also impact the DDT because the longer you work the dough, the greater the friction and the greater the heat output. You will find that duration plays a much more dramatic role with conventional kneading than with French kneading, once again because of the direct contact among the dough, hands, and work surface.

In addition, the temperature of the work surface is critical. If you are working on surfaces that are naturally cool to the touch, such as granite, then you are going to either have to increase your ambient air temperature or the temperature of your ingredients to ensure that the DDT is achieved. On the other hand, if you are working on a surface that more readily matches the ambient air temperature, such as wood, you will find that it is much easier to arrive at the DDT.

> The temperature of your work surface is particular to your kitchen, so I can't give you a precise measurement on the temperature of the air and ingredients. But do yourself a favor and feel the work surface before starting. It's part of the mental aspect of the *mise en place*, and it will help you determine how much you'll need to manipulate the other factors to arrive at the proper DDT.

It's important to understand that although all of this talk about DDT might be giving you horrid flashbacks to high school chemistry class, once you begin the process, you'll realize that it's quite easy to manage in the home bakery without a lot of thought or stress. In no time at all you'll be making adjustments on the go without much effort—mental, physical, or otherwise.

THE FINAL RESULT

By now, if you're anything like me, you're wondering what the final result of kneading should look like. The answer to this is both objective and subjective.

At the objective end of the spectrum, the answer is to perform what baker's call the "window test," which is used to assess whether proper gluten development has been achieved. Some dough require less of a window than others, meaning that certain dough must be worked to an advanced stage of gluten development (one in which the dough can be stretched until the window is razor thin) while other dough may be ready to bulk ferment (the next step in the bread-baking process) when it arrives at the state just before it passes the window test. But as a general rule, passing the window test is a solid way to assess whether the gluten has developed enough so that the kneading process can end.

The "window test" does not apply to all dough. Dough with a higher hydration level, such as those over 75 percent like *ciabatta*, don't require passage of the window test because the gluten will not be developed enough until it is worked during the bulk fermentation process. Likewise, enriched dough that is mixed by hand won't pass the test either; it is just way too stiff after mixing and kneading and will tear rather than stretch. But that's okay; that's what is supposed to happen for those types of dough.

Here's how to do it:

1. Gently pinch a small amount of dough between your index fingers and thumbs.

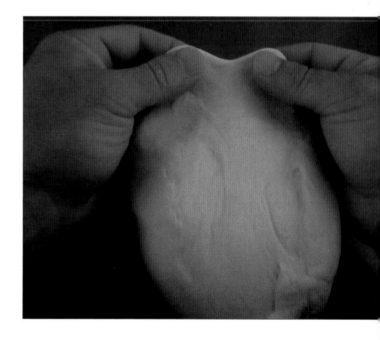

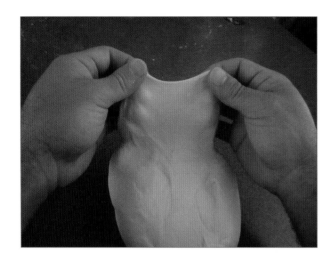

2. Tenderly stretch the dough, pulling upward and outward. The dough will become thinner and thinner, and if the gluten has been developed to the proper extent, you'll eventually be able to see through it just as if you were looking through a fogged-over pane of glass.

The subjective way of determining when the dough has been properly developed so that you may stop kneading is based upon nothing less than experience. And experience in this context refers to the feel of the dough. When the gluten has developed properly, it has an almost intangible quality to it that can only be understood by feeling the dough—maybe smooth and elastic are two words that come as close as any to describing the feel. And the only way to truly comprehend this subject method of determining gluten development in dough is to bake lots and lots and lots of bread. In the beginning, you will most certainly doubt yourself or second guess what you read or believe is accurate—I certainly did and continue to do

from time to time—but over time, you, like the professional baker, will be able to simply look at the dough, touch it, and know if it's ready for the next step.

If the dough feels brittle, it most likely needs additional work. Although, if you're working with whole wheat flour, the dough always has a certain roughness because of the hulls contained within the flour; and certain enriched dough, like brioche, that are mixed by hand are neither elastic nor brittle. But that's okay; it's supposed be that way. Also, if the surface of the dough appears to be smooth, it means you're farther along the path to proper gluten development. If not, keep kneading. But again, an exception can be made for whole wheat dough and some enriched dough.

You will read in many recipes not to overknead the dough. If you are using an electric mixer, this is a definite concern, but if you are kneading by hand, it's virtually impossible to overknead. Since the focus of this book is on hand-kneading, just keep working the dough until it has arrived at its proper stage of development.

Step Four: Bulk Fermentation

Once you've worked up the gluten in the dough, it's time to allow the yeast in the dough to ferment. This is accomplished during what bakers call bulk fermentation. You will see many cookbooks refer to this stage as the "first rise." They are just different names for the same thing.

Bulk fermentation is the point where the gases in the dough work within the internal structure created by the kneading process to expand the dough or cause it to rise. It is during this stage of dough development that the flavors of the dough come to life. This stage of the bread-baking process is of particular significance when preparing straight dough (or dough in which all the ingredients are mixed at once) because the dough will not have as much time to ferment and develop flavor as the dough prepared with a preferment (i.e., dough that incorporates a *biga* or *poolish*) or one prepared with a starter (i.e., sourdough). While the prefermented dough and sourdough starters have had anywhere from one to five days to develop the flavor that will ultimately be passed on to the dough in which it is utilized, straight dough usually takes no more than three to four hours to produce.

For many types of dough, the bulk fermentation process is as simple as this:

1. Lightly oil the container in which you will place your mixed and kneaded dough.

Because prefermented dough has a day or more to develop, it will require much less yeast than straight dough, which only has a few hours to develop its flavor.

The alcohol that is produced as a by-product during bulk fermentation helps to make the gluten more elastic, thus aiding in creating a higher quality internal structure in the dough.

2. Place the dough topside down inside the bowl so that it gets coated with oil.
3. Flip the dough over so that the top is now on top and gently push the sides of the dough against the container so that the entire surface of the dough has a light coat of oil on it.
4. Cover the container tightly with plastic wrap and place in a warm, draft-free area. (The location for your dough will be discussed below in greater detail.)

Some dough, mainly those with a higher level of hydration (those over 70 percent, such as *ciabatta* and some sourdough), require additional steps throughout the bulk fermentation process in order to aid in the distribution of the yeast and incorporate air into the dough. The latter will help the gluten strands to lengthen and thus produce greater internal structure within the dough. The technique for accomplishing this is called "folding." As you will see, the folding process also requires some shaping of the dough which, as it so happens, will give you a head start on understanding the preshaping and shaping discussions to come.

There are two ways to fold dough and both work equally well. Whichever you choose is simply a matter of personal preference. In that respect, give both a try and see which you like best.

Here's how to fold using the first method:

1. Scrape the dough out of the container and place it directly in front of you.

2. Gently stretch the dough into a square. (The dough has a tendency to return to its original shape, so just keeping working at it until you get it where you want it.)

3. Using both hands, pick up the right side of the dough and lift it off the work surface, stretching the dough upward as you lift (just don't tear it).

4. Fold the flap of dough one-third of the way across the square.

5. Repeat step 3 for the left side of the dough.

6. Fold the flap of dough across the rest of the dough.

7. Using both hands, pick up the end of the dough farthest from you and repeat step 3.

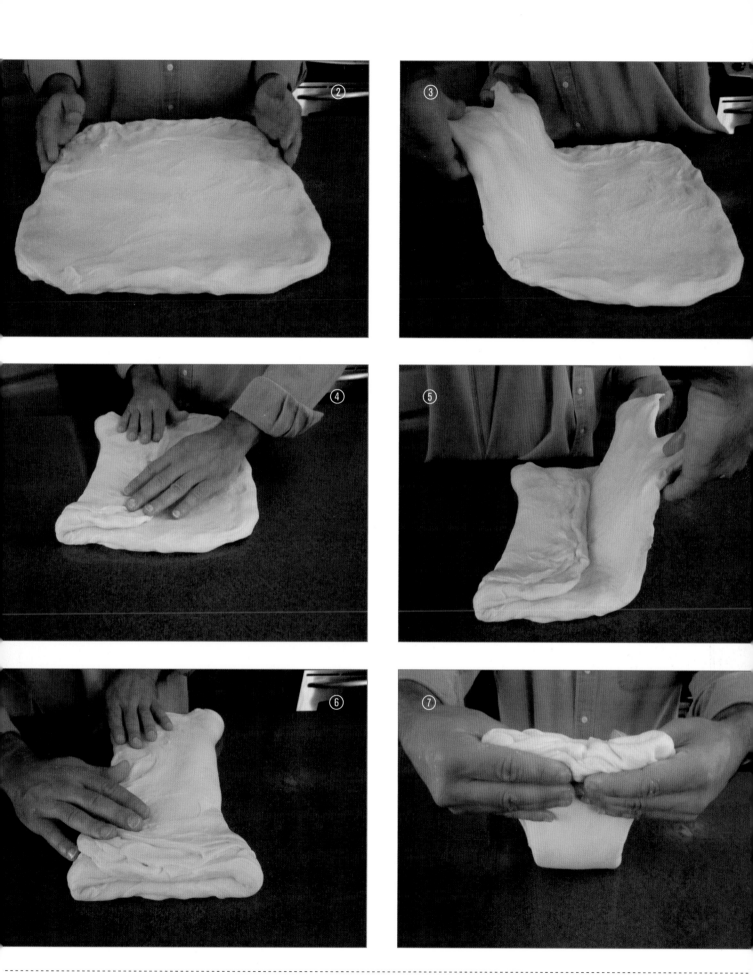

8. Fold the flap of dough one-third of the way across the dough.

9. Using both hands, pick of the end of the dough nearest to you and repeat step 3.

10. Fold the dough across the rest of the dough.

11. Flip the dough over so that what was once bottom of the dough is now the top. The surface of the dough will be shiny and smooth.

12. Place the dough about one foot away from your body and cup both hands around the dough so that your little fingers touch the work surface.

13. Drag the dough toward your body, making sure that the dough remains in contact with the work surface at all times. Friction is required in order for the dough to come together properly (so your work surface cannot have too much flour or oil on it or the dough will slide

too much). The bottom edge of the dough should become pinched between the work surface and your fingers. The top surface of the dough will begin to stretch and tighten (i.e., the surface of the dough will become more and more smooth).

14. Rotate the ball of dough about one-third of a turn, repeat steps 12 and 13. Then continue rotating the dough and performing steps 12 and 13 until all of the seams created by the folding are no longer visible and the dough comes together in the shape of a ball. (Notice the big air bubble on the right side of the photo near my thumb. This is a good sign and precisely what you're looking for.)

15. To further tighten the ball, cup your hands around both sides of the dough.

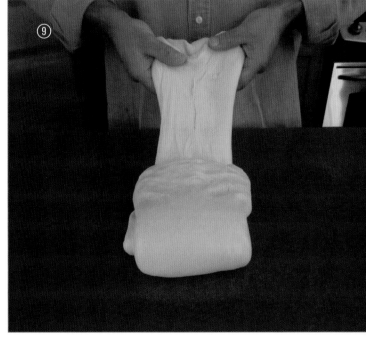

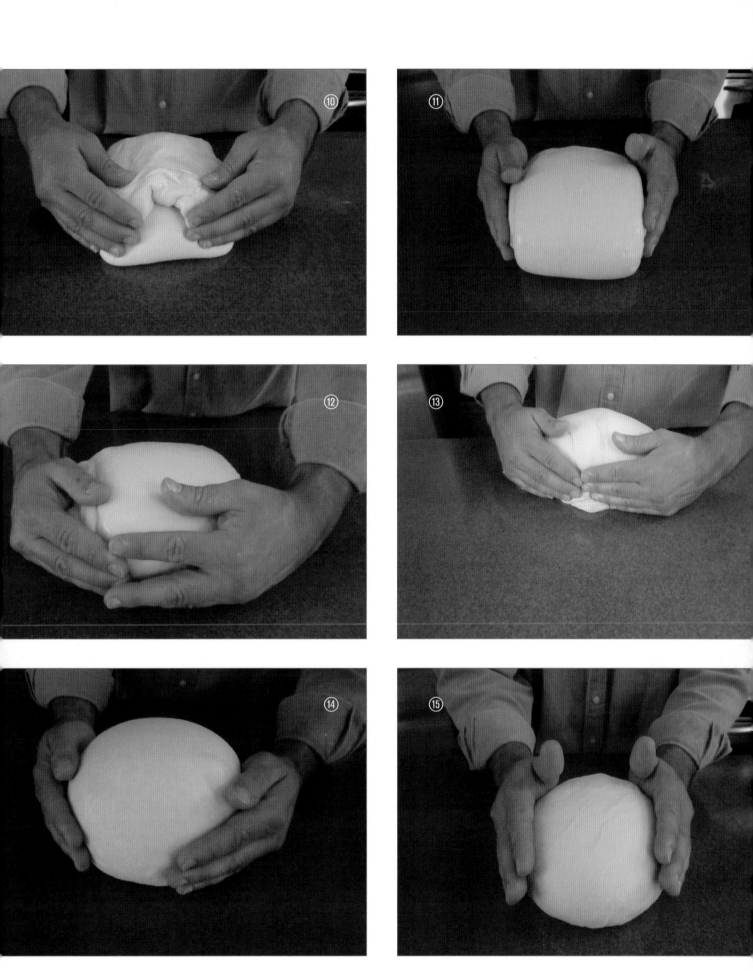

16. Lightly grip the dough (but enough so that the dough adheres to your hands) and stretch the surface of the dough downward.

17. Keep stretching—but don't tear—the surface of the dough until your hands are cupped underneath the dough, almost to its center, and your palms are facing up.

18. Rotate the dough and repeat until a nice, tight skin is formed across the ball.

19. The surface of the dough should look tight, and air bubbles should appear just beneath the surface. At this point, return the ball of dough to its container, cover it, and continue the fermentation process as described in the specific recipe.

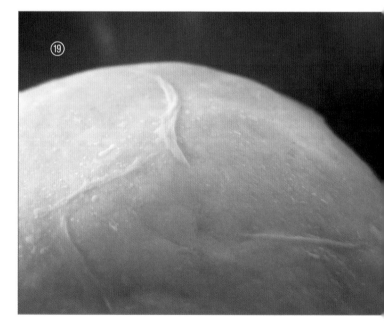

During the folding process, gluten is further enhanced, making for a chewier and less tough crumb.

Here's how to fold using the second method:

1. Scrape the dough out of the container and place it directly in front of you.

2. Place both hands under the right side of the dough.
3. Lift the dough upward and stretch it (but don't tear it) just as you did with the first method.
4. Fold the dough to the center of the rest of the dough.
5. Place your hands under the dough about 1/6 of the way around the rest of the dough.
6. Lift the dough upward and stretch it (but don't tear it) just as you did in step 3.

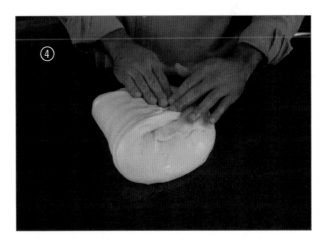

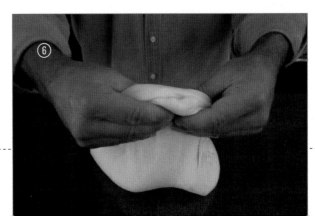

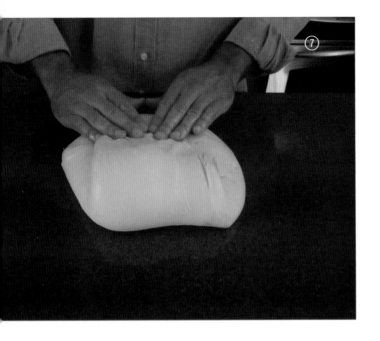

7. Fold the dough to the center of the rest of the dough. Move your hands another 1/6 of the way around the dough, and repeat steps 3 and 4. Make your way around the entire piece of dough. When done, flip the dough over so that what was once the bottom is now the top. Tighten the dough like you did in steps 12 through 18 of the first method. After completing that, your dough will look just like it did at the end of the first method (see photo of step 15 in the first method). At this point, return the ball of dough to its container, cover it, and continue the fermentation process as described in the specific recipe.

FOLDING TIPS

- If your dough is extremely wet (i.e., 75 percent or more hydration), then it helps to very lightly coat your work surface with oil to prevent the dough from sticking to the work surface. At this stage of the process, you do not want to incorporate any additional moisture into the dough, so use as little as possible to get the job done.

- Do not rip the dough during the folding process. It will damage the gluten strands that you've been so diligent in developing.

- Do not be afraid of the dough just because it's very loose in texture. You are not going to destroy it. By now it has a backbone of its own. The key is to use care just as you would with any living creature (and yes, dough is a living creature; if you don't believe it, just ask the yeast).

- When lifting, stretching, and folding the dough, it is better to think of the act as one smooth motion rather than three individual parts. This will allow you to work more efficiently and will make the entire process smoother.

- Do your best to fold the dough as prescribed above, but don't worry if your fold is a little off center. Dough is not the most cooperative thing in the world, so sometimes it's going to do what it wants to do. Give it some room, and send it some good vibes. It will eventually see that you know what you're doing, listen to your direction, and follow your lead. After all, isn't communication the key to success in virtually every aspect of life?

- The thickness of the dough that you stretch into the initial square will depend wholly upon the amount of dough you are working with. However, dough that is about 1,000 grams or less (two pounds or less) should be no less than three-quarters of an inch in thickness. Larger batches of dough (2,000-plus grams) will generally be around one and one-quarter inches in thickness. You will also find that the wetter the dough, the easier it is to stretch, and the thinner it will become.

- Some books will instruct you to fold the dough within the bowl you're proofing it in. Although it sounds simple, it's actually a bit tricky to get a grasp on enough dough to lift, stretch, and fold it when you're beginning and when you're not working with a larger container. I

recommend trying this method after you've mastered the others. Who knows, you might just find that this works great for you.

Punching down the dough, which is commonly prescribed in many older cookbooks, is now considered archaic and not recommended. The techniques described in this book replace punching down and produce much better results.

OIL VS. FLOUR

One of the age-old debates among bread bakers is whether to use oil, flour, or neither on the surface of the container you will use during bulk fermentation. Each has its pluses and minuses. As for oil, it is by far the best way to make sure that your dough does not stick to the sides of the container. However, as discussed above, use as little as possible because you do not want to incorporate extra moisture into the dough at this point.

What kind of oil should you use? Generally, flavorless oil works best, such as canola or vegetable. However, if you are making dough that uses a particular type of oil, such as olive oil in *focaccia*, then use that type of oil to lubricate your bowl (or work surface). That way the flavor will remain constant.

Flour is often used to lubricate a container during bulk fermentation. You'll see this most often with artisan bakers. Flour does work to prevent the dough from sticking to the surface of the container; however, as the hydration level in dough increases, flour becomes less and less effective. Rather than preventing sticking, it actually causes more sticking. And the goal is to keep the dough intact, not leave half of it in the bowl. Additionally, incorporating more flour into the dough is no more a good idea than incorporating more liquid because you don't want to interfere with the balance of ingredients that you so carefully weighed out earlier in the process. But if you have to choose, go with more moisture (oil).

Some artisan bakers are continually trying to push the limit on how much hydration they can incorporate into a recipe, and the quality of the end result is tough to argue with. So from this perspective, it makes sense that adding a bit of moisture from the oil is far better in the long run than reducing the overall hydration level by adding flour.

But there are those who don't oil or flour their containers. Sure, this may work with very low hydration level dough, but beyond that, it will cause you nothing but grief. I learned this the not-so-easy way. Since it's just not worth the madness avoiding flour or oil brings, use some sort of lubricant. The choice is yours, so feel free to experiment, but for me—oil wins out in my kitchen any day of the week.

PLASTIC WRAP VS. TOWELS

Here, we're talking about what to cover your container with. This really comes down to being able to keep the moisture in the container and, more important, in the dough. Many recipes in other books call for the use of a dry or damp towel. If you live in an environment with high humidity, such as the Southeastern United States, then a towel will probably work just fine. But if you bake in an arid climate, as are common in many parts of the Western United States, you will need, at a minimum, a damp towel. However, no matter what environment you live in plastic wrap is by far the covering of choice. It's cheap, flexible, and creates an airtight seal around the rim of the container. Because of this, use plastic wrap. This will give you one less thing to worry about in the bread-baking process.

If you'd prefer not to use a towel or you're against using plastic wrap, purchase an airtight container (i.e., one with a lid) for fermentation. Just make sure it's large enough to accommodate full expansion of the dough.

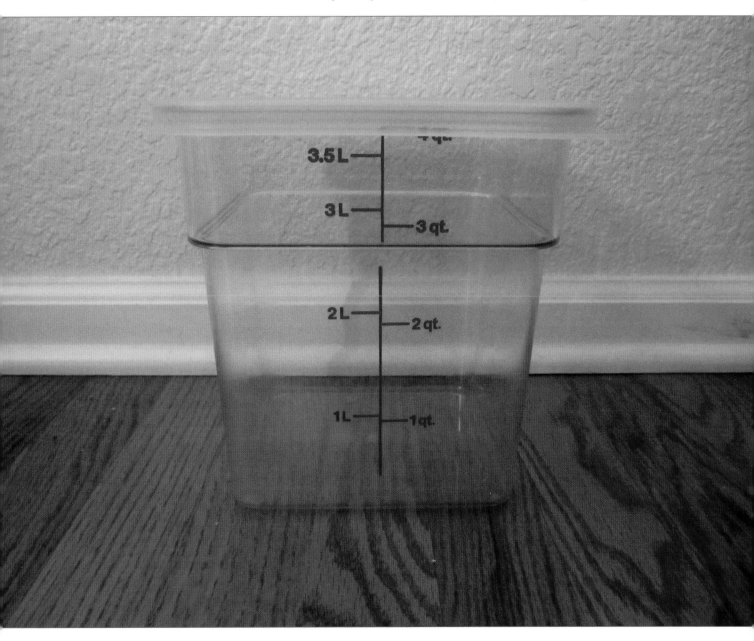

The reason that using the right material to trap moisture is so important is because if you use the wrong material and the dough dries a skin will develop on the dough. This skin will prevent the dough from expanding, which will produce a less than perfect product. This is not as much of a concern in more humid climates, but it definitely plays a role in dryer areas. And if a skin does appear to be developing on the dough, mist it lightly with water. The additional moisture will help to combat the skin development. Just be sure that when you cover the dough up, use plastic wrap lightly coated with oil so that the dough does not stick to the wrap if it touches it.

Yeast thrives in the 86°F–95°F range, but fermenting at that level would subtract from the flavor component of the bread, which develops better at lower temperatures. That's why you ferment at the lower temperatures. Ultimately, it's a balancing act between optimizing yeast activity and the taste of the bread.

TEMPERATURE AND HUMIDITY

Cookbooks are peppered with bread recipes that call for the baker to let the dough rise in a warm part of the kitchen, but they rarely if ever tell you what warm is. Ideally, for the professional baker, warm means 75°F–85°F for recipes that call for white and wheat flour and 80°F–90°F for those that require rye flour.

Now, unless it's summertime or you live in the Deep South, it's tough to maintain an ambient air temperature of 75°F in your kitchen all year round. What can you do to come as close to that 75°F mark in your kitchen when you just can't turn up the heat on your furnace? The answer for the professional baker is a proofing cabinet, which is a piece of equipment used extensively in commercial bakeries. (And even though it's called a proofing cabinet, it can just as easily be used to bulk ferment.) It looks like a very tall oven, is airtight, and allows the baker to control temperature and humidity after the dough is placed inside it. If you've got several thousand dollars lying around and an extra ten square feet of floor space, then I'd highly suggest purchasing one. However, if you're like me and most people I know, that isn't an option. Instead, I use a virtually free way to get around this that does not require any additional equipment.

THE HOMEMADE PROOFING CABINET

You can make your very own proofing cabinet using your oven. Since your oven is airtight for the most part when not turned on (when it's turned on, the ventilation system

One of the means to bulk ferment dough is to use the warmth of the sun, if it's strong enough, and if you're lucky enough to have it. But don't put the dough in direct sunlight. Rather, place it near a sunny spot so that it can absorb the radiant heat. If the temperature grows too warm—leave your chef's thermometer on the container to monitor it—move it to a cooler area. If the temperature is just right, sit back, and watch the miracle unfold (Just admit it: watching dough expand pretty cool!).

acts to expel moisture from its interior), it serves as the perfect enclosure for mimicking the professional-grade proofing cabinet. There are two ways to accomplish this. The first is by turning on the oven to its lowest setting. Once it reaches that temperature setting, turn it off, crack open the door, and allow the heat to escape. About fifteen minutes later (and this may take a little longer depending on how low you can set your oven), place your container of dough in the oven and close the door. The residual heat from the original heating of the oven will be enough to maintain a 75°F environment. If you find that it's too warm, open the door of your oven to allow

How to Monitor Heat During Bulk Fermentation and Proofing: Set a chef's thermometer on top of your proofing container and leave it there throughout the fermentation process. This will allow you to check the temperature of the surrounding area with nothing more than a quick glance.

additional heat to escape. If it's still too warm, open the door to allow the heat to escape and remove your container of dough and set it aside until the proper temperature is present.

> If the heat is too high, the yeast will kick into high gear (as long as the temperature remains below about 130°F), and you will overferment the dough. This will create nothing less than subpar, if not inedible, bread. The lesson: Pay close attention to the temperature of your fermentation area.

However, if you live in an environment with very low humidity, or you're finding that the dough is just not increasing in volume like it should, here's another trick that will help you get one step closer to creating a professional proofing cabinet. Add a pan of boiling water to the oven. This serves two purposes: one, the steam released from the water will create humidity, which will aid in the fermentation process, and two, the boiling water will give off additional heat that will keep your oven at the proper temperature for a longer period than if you were just relying on residual heat alone. But, as with regulating the temperature when you preheat the oven, you still need to monitor the temperature because the boiling water

may raise the temperature too much. So just keep an eye on it and open the oven door to release heat if necessary, or temporarily remove the dough until conditions are right.

> Make sure you have water boiling *before* you get to this stage so that in case you need some extra heat or moisture, it's ready to go.

The real concern with temperature and humidity is that you need to understand the nuances of your own kitchen. Where are the hot spots? Where is it drafty? Is it warmer in the morning or afternoon? Ponder these things as you bake and you'll quickly discover what works best in your kitchen.

DURATION AND RETARDING DOUGH

The duration of the bulk fermentation is provided in each recipe in this book and in virtually every book I've seen on the subject. However, duration is function of both time and volume. Most recipes will use both to dictate when bulk fermentation is complete. For example, many will state: Ferment until the dough is double in volume, about one hour. However, the main focus should be on volume, with time being only an approximation of when the desired dough volume will be achieved. The reason for this is because so many variables come into play, including temperature and humidity variations. But even more important is the effect of altitude on the duration of fermentation. As a general rule, the higher the altitude, the less time it will take for dough to increase to the desired volume level; at lower altitude, it will take very close to the time prescribed for the dough to rise to the required volume. For example, the recipes in this book were tested at an elevation of around 6,400 feet in the Rocky Mountains and at sea level in South Florida and the Florida Keys. Bulk fermentation (and proofing) took approximately 30–50 percent less time at high altitude (as long as the temperature remained around 75°F) compared to low altitude. This is a direct result of the lower atmospheric pressure present as altitude increases, which allows for greater expansion sooner. Because of this, it's important to pay attention to the volume of the dough rather than focus solely on the time prescribed in a recipe. And in the grand scheme of bread baking, it is always better to go with looks, feel, and experience over specific time instructions, whether

pertaining to bulk fermentation, proofing, or baking.

RETARDING DOUGH

As you advance in your bread baking, you will most definitely come across recipes that call for retarding the dough, or slowing down the fermentation process. Since dough develops its flavor during the bulk fermentation process, prolonging the process will create additional flavor in the dough, which will necessarily be imparted to the final product.

This method has become extremely popular in recent years and is mainly accomplished through refrigerating the dough during fermentation. Although refrigerating dough in quantities great enough for commercial bread production is impractical if not impossible, retarding dough through refrigeration is very much possible in the home bakery. So after you mix and knead the dough, place it in the refrigerator to ferment overnight. Pull it out in the morning and continue the rest of the baking process.

Be sure to make a mental note what the volume of the dough is before you begin bulk fermentation so that you can accurately judge when it's increased to its designated degree.

If there is an area of your house that is cool enough (one that remains in the 55°F or lower temperature), most likely in the winter months, you can leave your dough out on the counter rather than refrigerate it. This will accomplish the same effect as refrigeration.

Retarding dough can come in handy if you run out of time to finish the rest of the baking process. Just slip the dough in the refrigerator and remove it the next day when you're ready to continue.

The main thing to remember with retarding is that after you refrigerate the dough, you will have to allow the dough to return to room temperature (around 75°F) before you can continue working with the dough in the bread-baking process. If you work the dough too soon, it will impact the remainder of the process because the yeast will either not function properly because it has become dormant. So allowing the dough to return to the 75°F range will cause the yeast to reactivate itself from its dormancy and do what it's supposed to do.

Retarding dough is used mainly with straight dough because it does not have the benefit of a preferment such as *biga*, *poolish*, or a starter as is used with sourdough. Allowing the dough to refrigerate overnight will give it similar benefits as the preferments do.

Step Five: Pre-Shaping and Resting

Once your dough has fermented to the proper degree, it's time to preshape the dough and allow it to rest. Essentially, this step entails forming the dough into a shape that resembles the final shape, most often an oblong or a round. So you have to know what your final shape is going to be prior to preshaping. Most recipes will provide you with a final shape, but experience and imagination can also help make this determination.

Preshaping builds internal structure within the dough that gives the dough strength. This translates into bread that is not only tastier but more appealing to the eye. But it's not just about influencing the shape of the dough that's important here. There's another critical portion of this step whose importance cannot be overlooked or overstated.

Part of the preshaping process includes allowing the dough to rest—just letting the dough sit there without doing a thing to it once it's been preshaped. This causes the gluten strands within the dough to relax. Without relaxation, the dough would be much more difficult to manipulate during final shaping. Plus, it gives you fifteen to twenty minutes to reassess the mental aspect of your *mise en place* to make sure that you're geared up and ready for the next stage in the baking process.

When working with very wet dough, dip your scraper in a bowl of water before attempting to remove the dough from its container. It will help to prevent the dough from sticking to the scraper. (I've heard some bakers advocate using cooking spray; however, I've found that the alcohol content in the spray sometimes permeates the dough and leaves that unappealing flavor behind. Because of that, I suggest sticking with the water.)

However, before the dough can be preshaped, it has to be scaled, or weighed. Scaling is determined partly by recipe and partly by preference. For example, to make a brioche loaf formed from small rounds in a one-pound pan, each of the rounds must be around 60 grams for best results. That's determined by the recipe, and it works quite well. On the other hand, challah is braided and baked on a sheet pan. So, you can either have a long or short loaf of challah, depending wholly on your personal preference, and that preference will determine the weight of the strands used for braiding. But no matter what, any good recipe will provide you with scaling recommendations for the particular bread you're creating. And it's best to heed its advice until you have the knowledge and confidence to venture forth on your own.

Bear in mind that if you do deviate from what a recipe calls for in terms of weight, a less than perfect product may result. For example, if you make rolls too small, they may dry out. If you make the loaves too large, the exterior and the dough close to

How to Divide Dough: You might think that you can just eyeball it and cut the dough into perfectly even sections, and you just might be lucky enough to be able to. But here's a tip that will help you divide the dough more evenly on the first try. Gently form your dough into a round shape (after bulk fermentation and before preshaping). Then envision the face of a clock on the surface of the dough and use the hours as natural divisions on the dough. For example, if you want three pieces, make your cuts at the twelve, four, and eight o'clock positions. If you want four pieces, make cuts at the twelve, three, six, and nine o'clock positions. Although it's by no means perfect, this method will help you get much closer than if you just randomly eyeballed it.

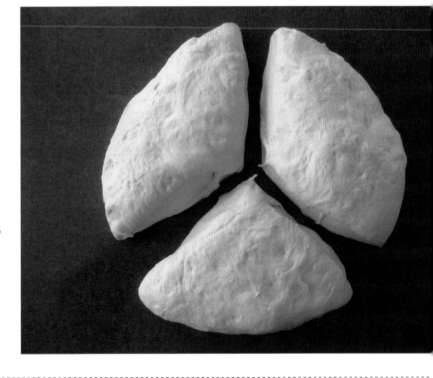

the exterior may be baked perfectly, but the interior may be underbaked. My suggestion is to follow the professional bakers' instructions until you become comfortable with the recipe, mainly after baking the bread several times. Once you arrive at that level of familiarity with the dough, feel free to experiment.

Nevertheless, the truth is unless you deviate drastically from a recipe, the bread will still be edible. It might not be perfect, but you won't have to throw it out. In this respect, perform your shaping experiments in incremental stages. This means that if a recipe calls for 75-gram pieces, but you feel these are just too large for your needs, don't just cut the weigh down to 40 grams. Reduce it down to 60 grams then to 55, 50, and so on until you arrive at the perfect size for your purpose. The more substantial the immediate deviation, the greater the likelihood that you'll be filling your trash bin with something that you shouldn't have had you

been a bit more reserved in manipulating the advice of the pros. Moral of the story: small changes make for less disappointment. Trust me—and my garbage can—throwing dough in the trash is not a confidence builder, and even more, it's a disgraceful waste of food.

Now, once you've settled on a final shape and size for your dough, you'll find preshaping is divided most commonly into two shapes—round loaves and oblong loaves—since these two forms largely encompass, or roughly resemble, what will eventually become the final shape of the bread.

Here's how to preshape a round using the first method:

1. Place your dough in front of you and, using your bench knife, cut the dough, and scale it.
2. Position the longer side of the dough parallel to you and place your fingers under the right half of the dough.

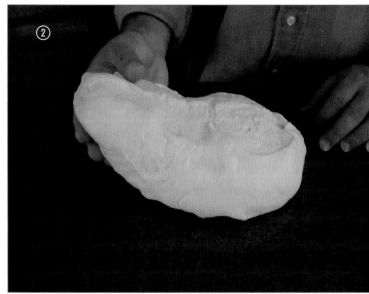

3. Fold the dough in half.
4. Using your side of your thumb, press down on the edge of the dough (but don't crush it) to seal the top and bottom edges together.
5. Repeat step 4 until the entire edge of the dough is sealed.
6. Rotate the dough 90 degrees, repeat steps 2 through 5, and then refer to steps

12 through 15 in the first method of folding to tighten the dough. Once complete, cover the dough and allow it to rest.

To preshape a round using the second method, refer to the second method of folding and repeat the entire process; it's that simple. Plus, you don't have to learn a

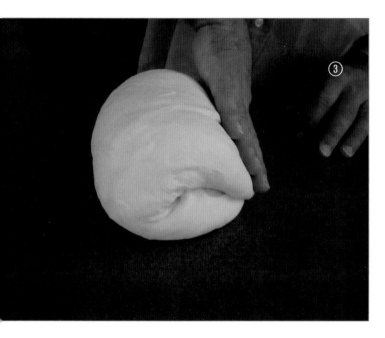

new skill. That said, I still find that the first method of preshaping a round works the best. But I encourage you to try them both to see which works best for you.

If you are working with more than one piece of dough, keep track of which one you worked on first because when you advance to the next stage—final shaping—you will shape the dough in the same order. This ensures greater uniformity because each piece of dough will be given the same amount of time to rest.

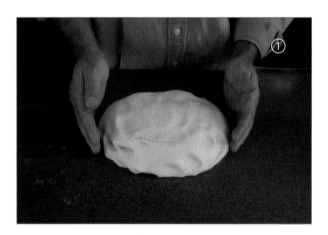

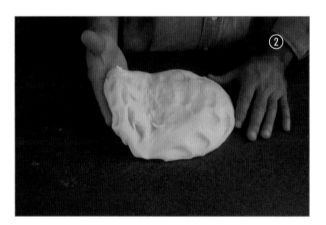

Here's how to shape an oblong:

1. Position dough in front of you with the longer side of the dough parallel to you.
2. Place your fingers under the right side of the dough.
3. Fold the dough to the center of the rest of the dough.
4. Place your fingers under the left side of the dough.
5. Fold the dough to the edge of the opposite fold.
6. Place your fingers under the edge of the dough farthest from you.
7. Fold the dough 1/3 of the way down the rest of the dough.
8. Use the side of your thumb to seal the edge of the dough to the rest of the dough.
9. Place your fingers under the top half of the dough.
10. Fold the dough in half and use the side of your thumb to seal the edges of the dough together.
11. Place the dough seam-side down, cup your hands over the top of the dough, and gently rock it back and forth to tighten the dough. Set the dough aside, cover it, and allow it to rest.

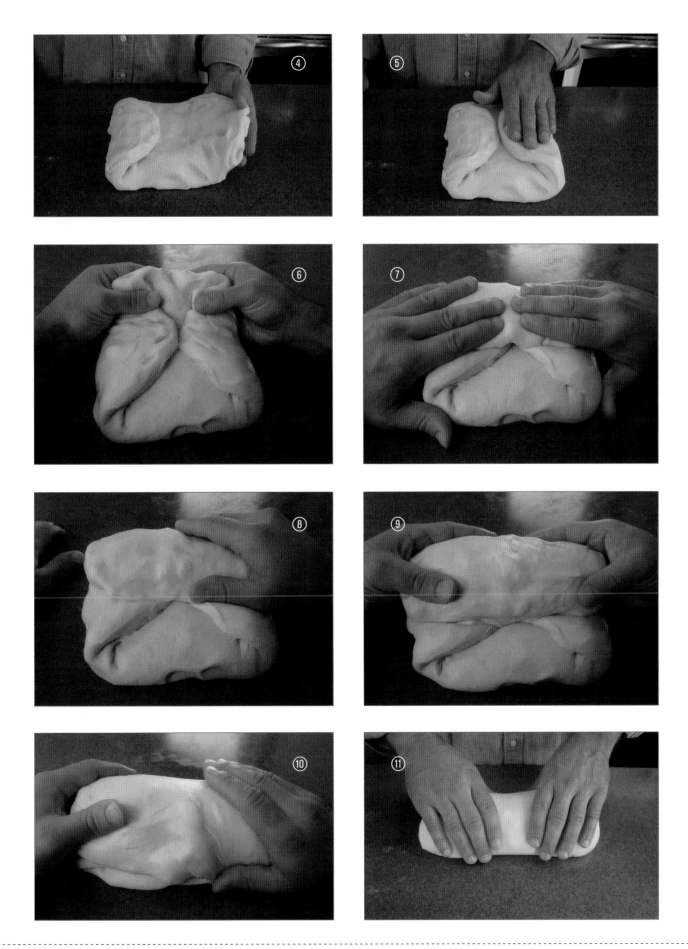

TIPS FOR PRESHAPING

- When scaling, don't be afraid to add or subtract pieces of dough to make sure that all of your pieces are of equal weight. This is particularly true when forming smaller items, such as rolls. Eventually, you'll get better at estimating and cutting the dough closer—and even dead-on— to the precise size you desire.

- Although you can use a sharp knife to cut the dough, a bench knife performs the job so much more easily. It's simply a matter of using the right tool for the job. Plus, you can then use the bench knife to slide under the dough to move it to wherever you need to on your work surface.

- When using your thumb to seal the edges of the dough together, be firm but do not crush the dough. Although the dough has developed internal structure by this stage, it still must be handled with care. So when sealing the edges, it might help to think of it more in terms of merging the two edges rather than forcing them to become one. The good news about this procedure is that, as with most, you'll get better with practice.

- For larger loaves (around two pounds), the oblongs will be 8 to 10 inches in length. For smaller loaves (like baguettes or strands for braiding), the oblongs will be about five inches in length.

THE BENCH REST

The bench rest follows preshaping. It's an essential step to ensure that the dough is ready to move on to the final shaping in the next stage of the bread-baking process. It's about as simple of a process as can be imagined in terms of execution since all you do after you have preshaped the dough is place it on your work surface, cover it, and allow it to sit without harassing it. It's kind of like a mini vacation for the dough after bouts of being roughed up during preshaping and final shaping. However, although it's easy to mechanically carry out, there are a few things to keep in mind when bench resting.

> The duration of the bench rest is directly proportional to the quality of your preshaping. The better the preshape, the longer it can rest. So take your time with preshaping and do it right. It makes for a more efficient home bakery.

Time and temperature are the main considerations. For most recipes, a bench rest of 10–20 minutes is prescribed. This provides the dough with enough time for the gluten to relax, as discussed above, so that the dough can then be given its final shape. The temperature of the area should be around 75°F, the same temperature that's desired for bulk fermentation. Although creating this temperature environment is ideal, for those of you who are baking a cooler environment, it might be tough to achieve. But don't worry, the bench rest lasts for such a relatively short period of time when compared to bulk fermentation, and proofing that a few minutes in a cooler environment won't have that much of an impact. The more important aspect is the fact that the dough is resting without being worked. That's the part that's most valuable in the grand scheme of bread baking.

Depending on the temperature and humidity of the area in which you are bench resting your dough, you may have to use some type of lubricant on the work surface to make sure that the dough does not stick to the work surface. As discussed in the bulk fermentation section, flour or oil are your ingredients of choice. If necessary, use whichever one works best for you— although I'd definitely recommend the oil—but no matter what, use as little as possible to get the job done. Again, you don't want to incorporate any additional flour or moisture into the dough at this point since, if done in too extreme a measure, it will impact the hydration level of the dough.

> If you do have to use a bit of flour to lubricate your work surface, don't stick your hand directly in the flour bag. Use a scoop to prevent contamination.

Another issue to consider is what you should cover the dough with during the bench rest. You have three options: a towel, a couche, or plastic wrap. The dough needs to be covered so that the surface of the dough does not dry out and form a skin, or membrane, which will retard the dough's ability to expand. What you cover it with is largely a matter of the humidity level of the area in which you are baking. The lower the humidity, the greater the chance of a membrane forming on the exterior of the dough whereas the higher the humidity, the greater the chance of the dough sticking to the item you're covering the dough with. This means that a balance must be achieved.

A cotton towel works well in a moderately humid environment, and it can work well in higher humidity if you first coat the towel with flour before placing it over the dough. Similarly, you can use a *couche*. The fibrous nature of the linen makes it less prone to sticking to the dough than a cotton towel. But because the *couche*, like the cotton towel, has holes in it—even with a heavy coating of flour—the dough is more prone to drying out on the surface in lower humidity environments. And remember, too much flour can result in more rapid drying of the dough surface.

> If you find that your dough is developing a skin, lightly mist it with water. This will help keep the moisture high enough to prevent that unwanted membrane from forming.

> If you proof your baguettes in a *couche*, proof them seam-side up. This way, when you flip them over onto the flipping board to move to the oven, they are right-side up.

Lastly, there is plastic wrap, which is ideal in both low- and high-humidity environments as the plastic acts as a vapor barrier, thus retaining moisture for the dough beneath it. However, since plastic wrap can be very clingy, it helps to very lightly coat the plastic wrap with oil, particularly in higher humidity climates. This will prevent the dough from sticking to its surface. Although a cotton towel and a *couche* can work very well, I've found that plastic wrap is by far the best choice. The only downside to plastic wrap is that it's disposable, so it's not great for the environment. But I've found that I can either use the same plastic wrap I used for bulk fermentation during the bench rest or I can reuse pieces of plastic wrap I've used in the past during the bench rest. This cuts down on waste and saves you money, so give it a try.

> Regardless of which material you choose to cover your dough with during the bench rest, make sure that you do not cover it too tightly. Doing so will prevent the dough from expanding naturally and thus subtract from the quality of the loaf you pull from the oven.

Step Six: Final Shaping

After the bench rest, it's time to create the final shape of the dough, which is what the dough will look like once you pull it from the oven. But in addition to simply providing a form for the dough, proper shaping helps to tighten up the dough, which will cause proofing, or the final rise time, and oven spring, or the dough's initial rapid rise while in the oven, to be that much more effective.

Although there are numerous shapes that encompass all of the breads of the world, there are four that will impart to you enough knowledge to make the vast majority of bread. They are the *boule* (round), *batard* (oblong), baguette (long and thin), and rectangular loaf (for a pan).

Before you begin final shaping, remember that the dough is a bit more delicate than it was previously. Because of this, handle the dough with care—i.e., don't beat it up or you'll destroy the internal structure and those wonderful gas pockets that you worked so hard to create in the first place.

SHAPING THE BOULE

A final *boule* shape is formed from the round preshape that was described previously. Although you may wonder why a piece of dough that has already been preshaped into a round needs to be shaped again into a round, there's a good reason for it. It might best be likened to participating in a sporting event. Preshaping is like warm-ups; it gets you ready for the important part that comes next—the game. When it comes to bread, final shaping is the game, and my guess is that if you've made it this far in this book, there's no doubt you want to win, so let's get to the final shaping of the *boule*.

Here's the easy part about shaping a *boule*: it's performed in precisely the same manner as the tightening process described in steps 15 through 18 of the first method of folding (pages 62–64). Just remember to use a round preshape to work with. Other

than that, follow those steps and you've got yourself a *boule*. This technique will serve you perfectly when you are craving a one- to two-pound *boule*—a perfect size for almost any taste—but if you want to mold your dough into rolls, then the technique changes just a bit.

> If you accidentally compress dough to the point where the internal structure is destroyed, don't worry. It's not ruined. You'll just have to take a step backward and allow the dough to rise again, kind of like repeating the bulk fermentation phase. Once you do, you'll be able to jump back in right where you left off. And because the dough will be fermenting longer than expected, more flavor will develop, so it's got it's upside, too (not that I recommend smashing your dough just to derive more flavor from it; there are easier ways to accomplish that).

First of all you will need to make sure that you scale your dough properly during your initial scaling prior to bulk fermentation. A common weight for a roll is around 50 grams, which will create a roll the size of a racquetball. Adjust the weight accordingly if you'd like to make them larger for submarine sandwiches or hoagies.

Although size in this instance is a function of how you intend to consume the bread, the key to remember is that all of the rolls must be the same weight and shape in order for them to bake properly. So, after accurately weighing them, here's what you do:

1. Place the small piece of dough in front of you. (If you have a small round already shaped, perfect. Here, you see a piece of brioche dough, which doesn't get preshaped. It's easier to see the process in action with a piece of dough that has not been preshaped. What's more, this technique comes in handy for preshaping small rounds, too.)
2. Place your fingers around over and around the dough. Make sure that your fingers are evenly spaced around the dough. Then move the dough in a small counterclockwise circle (if using your right hand).
3. As you apply light to medium pressure on the dough, it will begin to round. At this point, your fingers will tend to widen, rather than remaining pressed against the dough. Your palm will be doing a majority of the work by now. Without squeezing the dough, rotate your hand (along with the dough) in a circular motion. You will feel the dough stretching against the work surface and against your fingers.
4. Continue rotating the dough in a circle until the surface of the dough tightens and forms a nicely shaped ball.

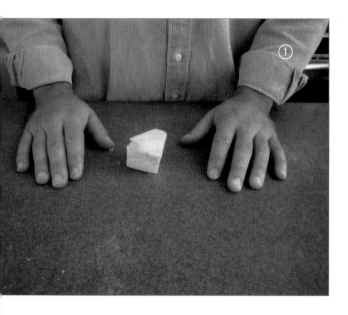

The ideal shape.

TIPS FOR SHAPING A ROLL

- If your finished rolls are coming out misshapen, use a bit more pressure with your fingers on the sides of the dough and press down slightly more on top of the dough. This will create greater friction for the dough against the work surface, which will cause the surface of the dough to tighten up more readily to produce a snug round roll.

- When you try this for the first time, shape one roll at a time. However, as you get more comfortable with the process, you'll be able to use both hands at once, which will increase your efficiency and get those rolls in your mouth and belly sooner.

- Depending on the size of your hand, you'll discover that there is a maximum size that you can shape using this technique. If the dough is too large for your hand, simply revert to the two-handed method for shaping a *boule*.

SHAPING THE BATARD

The *batard* is the classic oblong loaf that we see so often in everything from supermarkets to artisanal bakeries. It is shaped from the oblong preshaping that was discussed earlier. The final shaping technique is similar to the preshaping but includes enough twists to make it unique.

To shape a *batard*:

1. Place the preshaped oblong in front of you with the longer side parallel to you.

2. Press down lightly on the dough to expel the unwanted gases.
3. Place your fingers underneath the top edge of the dough.
4. Fold the top edge of the dough 1/3 of the way down the rest of the dough. Then seal the edge with the side of your thumb.
5. Place your fingers underneath the upper corners of the dough.
6. Fold the corners diagonally toward the sealed edge of the dough. Then rotate the dough 180 degrees, and repeat steps 4–6.

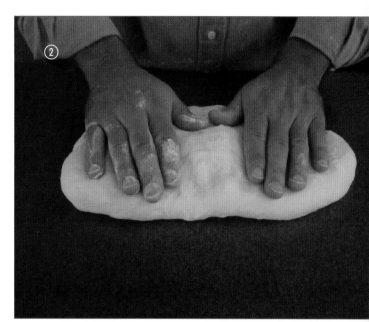

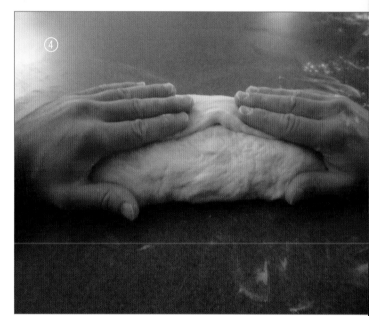

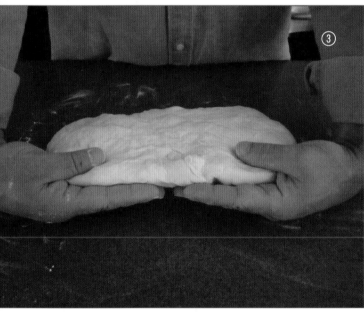

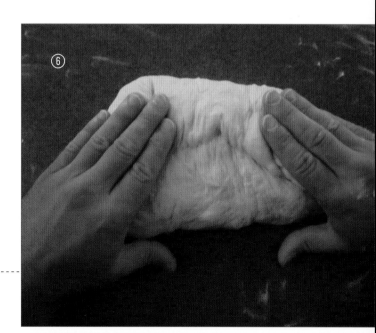

7. Place your fingers under the top edge of the dough.

8. Fold the top edge of the dough down to the bottom edge and, using the side of your thumb, seal the entire edge of the dough together.

9. Position the dough seam-side down, place your hands on top of the dough, and gently roll the dough back and forth

to tighten it. Gradually move your hands toward the ends of the dough. As your hands near the ends of the dough, close your fingers a bit more and exert a little more pressure to maintain the blunt but rounded end of the dough.

10. A nicely shaped *batard* (resting on a floured peel and ready for proofing).

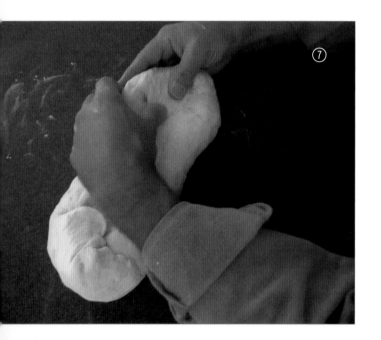

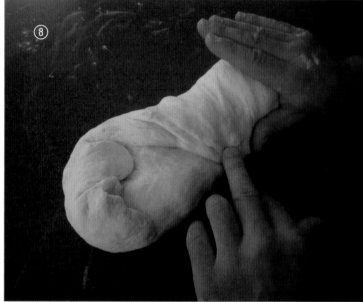

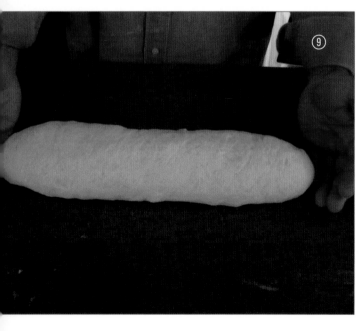

Softly patting the dough with the palm of your hand—commonly called degassing—before beginning to shape will help to remove the undesired carbon dioxide that has become trapped in the dough. Just don't deflate the dough in its entirety. Doing so gently is key.

TIPS FOR SHAPING A BATARD

- At first, shaping a *batard* is going to feel very mechanical. But with time you'll be able to shape this loaf in less than fifteen seconds.

- Be sure to fold enough of the corners of the dough toward the center of the dough, or you will end up with more of a rectangular loaf than an oblong loaf.

- With time, you will get a better feel for how much pressure to exert as you roll your hands on top of the dough and toward the edges. Be gentle at first because you don't want to crush the dough. But if you see that your dough is just not taking shape, use a little more pressure and see how that works. Again, this is all about feel, and that quality increases the more you bake.

SHAPING A BAGUETTE

Ah, the baguette—that ubiquitous shape that all of us love (and if you don't love it, you'd better learn to real fast!). Upon browsing through books on baking, you'll discover that bakers form baguettes in many different ways; however, the technique I present below is the most common.

Baguettes come in many lengths, from the mini baguettes that are only a half-dozen or so inches in length to the three-foot varieties you see in some bakeries. The length is a function of two considerations: taste and how big your oven is. Although I'd love to be able to bake the yard-long loaves, my oven (and baking stone) will only accommodate twenty inches at most. Ah, if only . . .

Here's how to shape a baguette:

1. Place a preshaped oblong piece of dough in front of you with the longer side parallel to you and gently pat it to expel unwanted gases that have built up within the dough.
2. Fold the top edge of the dough 1/3 of the way down the dough and, using the side of your thumb, seal the top edge of the dough to the rest of the dough, working down the entire length of the dough.
3. Rotate the dough 180 degrees and repeat step 2.
4. Your dough should look like this.
5. Fold the top edge of the dough to the bottom edge and, using the side of your thumb, seal the edges.
6. Continue sealing down the entire length of the dough.

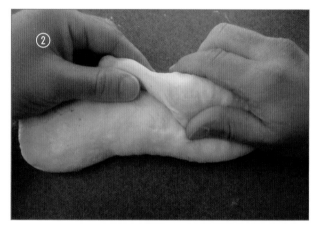

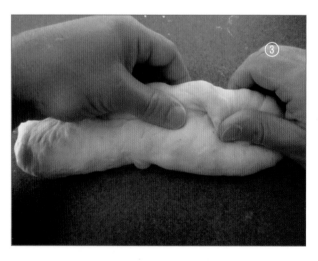

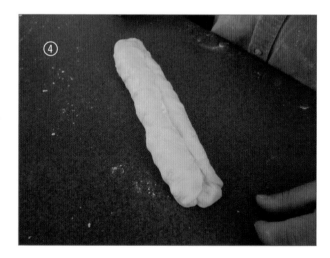

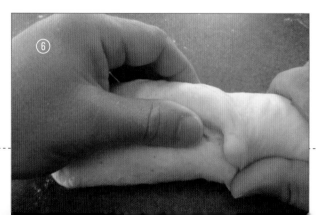

7. Position the dough seam-side down and place your hands on top of the dough. The tips of your fingers should be touching the work surface. Roll the dough back and forth, exerting downward and outward pressure to lengthen to dough to the desired degree. Be sure to apply even pressure so that the baguette maintains its shape, and apply a bit more pressure at the ends to taper the dough.

8. The dough should end up 1 1/2 to 2 inches in diameter (depending on how large you want the baguette to be). Notice the air bubble on the surface of the dough. This indicates nice structure within the dough.

9. Place the baguettes seam-side up between folds in a *couche* to proof.

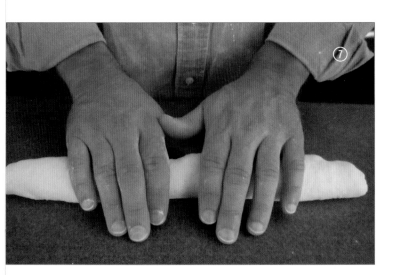

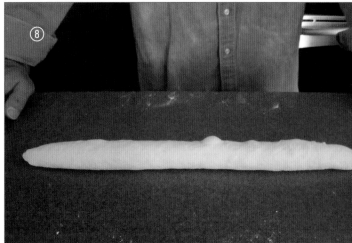

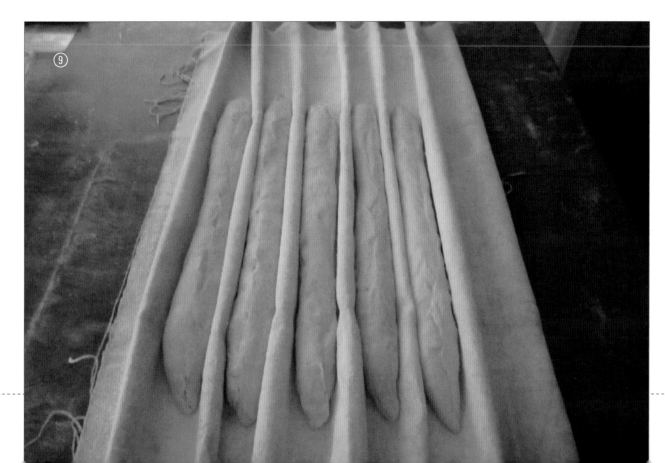

3. Place your fingers under the top edge of the dough and fold it in half so that the top edge of the dough is resting on the bottom. Then, using the side of your thumb, seal the edges of the dough together down the entire length of the dough.

4. Position the dough seam-side down and place your hands on top of the dough. Your fingers should be touching the work surface.

5. Roll the dough back and forth, exerting downward and outward pressure with your hands, until you achieve your desired length. The dough should be about 1 1/4 inches in diameter, and the ends of the dough should be tapered.

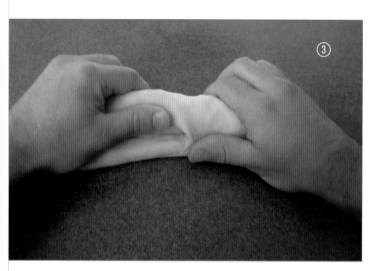

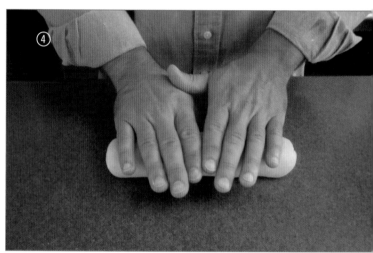

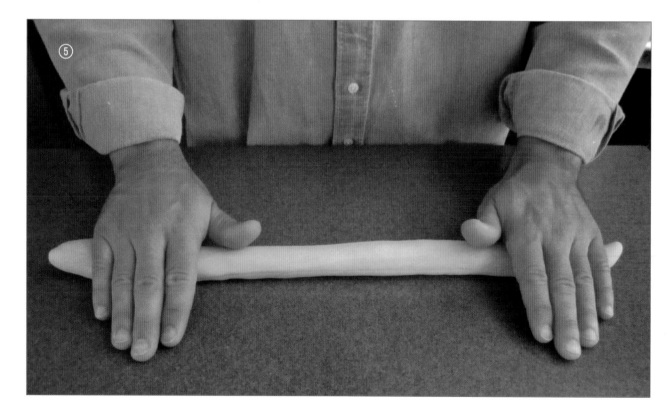

TIPS FOR SHAPING STRANDS

- You will notice that challah and brioche, which can both be braided, are enriched dough, so the dough will be much more firm than lean dough. Because of its firmness, it's more stubborn to work with, meaning it doesn't take shape as easily. To combat this, you'll have to use more pressure to get it in the form you need.

- It is of utmost importance to make sure that all of your strands are the same length. If they are not, there will be stray ends hanging out at the end of the braid. It will cause uneven baking, and it will subtract from visual appeal. And since we all know how much vision plays a role in the way something tastes, don't neglect this point and compromise all your hard work.

- The length of the strand will be determined by the recipe, but the most common length is around twenty inches. This gives you enough length to comfortably work with when it comes time to braid.

- The strands will not be proofed individually. They will first be braided, and then the braided loaf will be proofed.

BRAIDING THREE STRANDS

Although you can braid six strands or more, here's how to braid three strands, which is a common number and works well for virtually any purposes:

1. Place the 3 equal-length strands parallel to one another with the ends nearest to you. Lightly flour the surface of the strands.

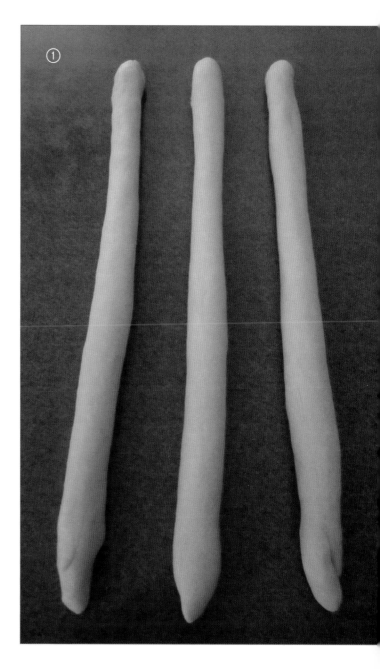

2. Beginning halfway down the length of the strands, lift the right strand over the center strand.

3. Lift the left strand over what is now the center strand.

4. Lift the right strand over what is now the center strand.

5. Repeat steps 3 and 4 until the strands are braided all the way to the end. Pinch the ends of the strands together and tuck them underneath the end of the braid.

6. Rotate the dough 180 degrees and repeat steps 2 through 5.

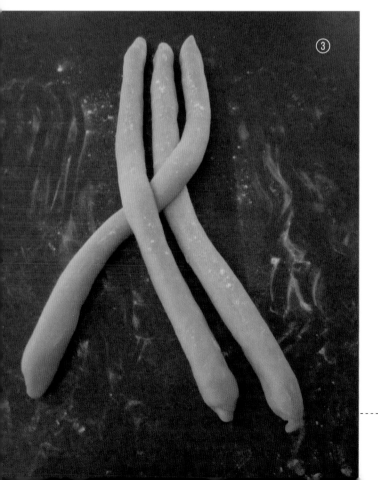

TIPS FOR BRAIDING

- Very lightly flouring the strands will help to keep them from sticking during the braiding process, and they will also aid in keeping the strands distinct during baking.
- Make sure that your strands are braided snugly. This will help to ensure that the dough maintains a uniform shape throughout the proofing and baking stages.
- Pay close attention to sealing the ends of the dough together and tucking them under the rest of the dough. If you don't, the braid may unravel during proofing and the initial stages of baking.

- Be careful when you move the dough to the surface upon which you will proof it. You don't want the braids to unravel or tear during the process. Using a large spatula or a bench knife can help in moving the dough.

Close-up of braids on challah.

The result of poorly sealed braids.

SHAPING A FOUGASSE

The *fougasse* is a leaf-shaped loaf of bread that is very common in many parts of France. Although recipes vary from region to region, baguette dough is widely used in shaping *fougasse*, and the general shape of the *fougasse* remains constant throughout the country (even though most bakers put their unique twists on it).

Here's how to shape it:

1. Place a preshaped round piece of dough in front of you.

2. Lightly pat the surface of the dough to expel the unwanted gases.

3. Gently stretch the dough until it resembles the shape of a large leaf.

4. Using a small scraper, make a cut all the way through the dough near the pointed edge of the dough, about an inch from the edge of the dough.

5. Continue cutting down the center of the dough until you are approximately an inch from the end of the dough.

6. Make an angular cut, about 35 to 40 degrees off the center cut, stopping an inch before the end of the dough. Do not let the angular cut intersect the center cut.

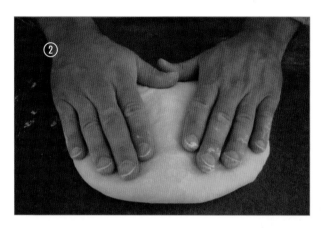

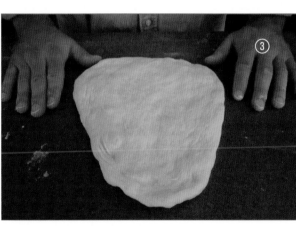

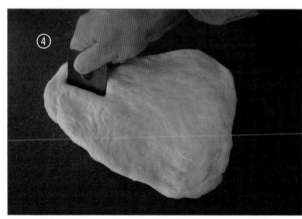

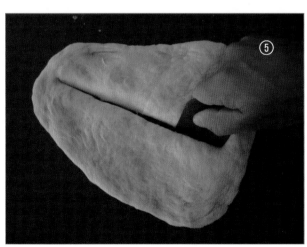

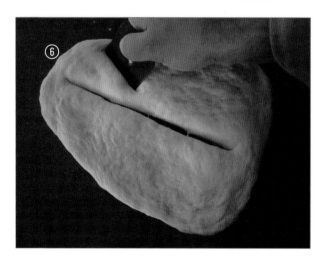

7. Repeat step 6 two more times down the right side of the dough, making each cut longer than the next so it is proportionate with the width of the dough.

8. Repeat steps 6 and 7 on the left side of the dough, then gently stretch the dough to open up the cuts.

9. After greasing a baking pan with butter and dusting it with cornmeal, place the *fougasse* on it, cover it, and allow it to proof.

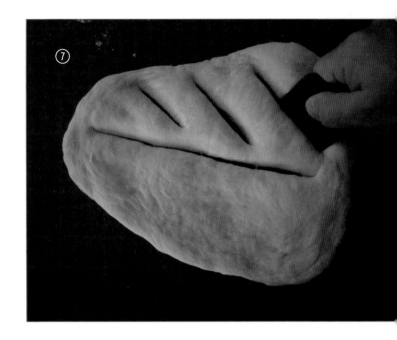

TIPS FOR SHAPING FOUGASSE

- Stretch the *fougasse* into its final form on the surface on you intend to proof and bake the dough—most often a baking sheet. If you try to lift the *fougasse* from the work surface and place it directly onto a baking stone, the dough will become misshapen and may tear.

- The thickness of the *fougasse* depends on your vision for the final product and the size of the dough. But, as a general rule, I've found that the texture of the final product becomes tougher the thinner the dough. For the most part, don't venture thinner than ¾ of an inch.

- The best tool to use to cut the *fougasse* is a small bowl scraper. Its compact size and overall stiffness make it perfect for the more precise cutting required for this shape. If you don't have a small bowl scraper, use a paring knife. It's not ideal, but if you're careful and diligent, you can get the same effect. Another option is to use the shorter end of your larger bowl scraper. The edge is a little long, but you can still make do if necessary.

SHAPING AN ÉPI DE BLÉ

The *épi de blé*, or *épi* for short, is bread that is shaped like a sheaf of wheat and is also commonly formed

from baguette dough. This shape serves a wonderful purpose in terms of being a unique and rather tasty way to eat a baguette. The small leaves can be broken off of the final product, slathered with butter, and enjoyed in one bite (well, at least if you have a mouth the size of mine!). But enough about what it is. Let's talk about shaping it.

To shape an *épi*:

1. After following the procedure for shaping a baguette, place the shaped baguette in front of

you with the longer side of the dough parallel to you. Then, with a sharp pair of scissors, cut the dough at an approximately 30 degree angle to the work surface and about ¾ of the way through the dough. Do not cut through the entire piece of dough.

2. Move the cut piece of dough to the right side of the dough, using care not to rip the piece from the rest of the dough.

3. Repeat step 1, and move the piece of dough to the left side of the dough.

4. Repeat this process down the entire length of the dough.

TIPS FOR SHAPING AN EPI

- The first time you do this you're likely going to be a little hesitant. Don't be afraid. Just cut. What's the worst that can happen? You accidentally cut off a leaf and end up with a mini, mini baguette? That's not a bad penalty for such an error.

- Use a shallow angle with scissors, which will help each of the wheat florets (the pieces that look like individual leaves) look more distinct when they come out of the oven.

- Quick cuts with the scissors are better than slow cuts. Slow cuts may snag the dough, which might cause the dough to become misshapen.

- As with the *fougasse*, cut your *epi* on the surface that you plan to proof and bake the *epi*. Attempting to move it will most likely lead to physical breakdown of the *epi* and mental breakdown of the baker.

SHAPING CIABATTA

Ciabatta is bread that is shaped like a slipper (That's what *ciabatta* means in Italian.). This dough is shaped with minimal amounts of manipulation. The reason for doing this is to avoid destroying the huge holes that the baker has so painstakingly worked to develop in the crumb. Also, note that *ciabatta* is not preshaped. You'll be working the dough straight out of its bulk fermentation container.

Here's how to form it:

1. Cut and scale the dough to the desired size. Just be very gentle with it when you are handling it.

2. Lightly stretch the dough into the shape of a rectangle. The dough has a tendency to spring retract to its original form, so be prepared to work with it to stretch it a bit farther each time it retracts.

3. The final product should be a rectangle with slightly rounded corners, just like a slipper.

4. Softly move the dough onto a *couche*, cover it, and allow it to proof.

TIPS FOR SHAPING CIABATTA

- Take your time with this one. If you work too fast, I guarantee you will damage the internal structure of the dough to one degree or another.

- When the time arrives to transfer this dough to a peel (you'll flip it over to do this), be gentle but deliberate in moving it so that you don't accidentally tip it on its side and crush it. One motion works best.

- Keep in mind that this shape is meant to look rustic, so a little dent here or there will give it character.

SHAPING FOCACCIA

This dough is pretty forgiving in its handling. It's shaping is divided into two parts: initial shaping and dimpling. The reason for this division is because the dough will need to proof after initial shaping and before dimpling, which will occur immediately prior to baking. So the proofing acts as somewhat of an intermediate stage in the final shaping process when compared to the one-step final shaping that occurred with the other dough that's been covered.

Here's how to perform the initial shaping:

1. Place a preshaped round on a lightly greased baking sheet or a baking sheet lined with parchment paper.
2. Using your fingers, stretch and slide the dough toward the sides and ends of the sheet pan.
3. Be sure that the dough stretches all the way to the sides and corners and that the dough is even in thickness throughout. Cover the dough and allow it to proof.

Here's how to dimple the dough:

1. After the dough has proofed, position the sheet pan in front of you and gently push your fingertips into the dough. Do not crush the dough; rather, try to make indentations in the dough.

2. Continue this process over the entire area of the sheet pan. There should be plenty of dimples, but not so many that they are running into one another.

Notice the randomly scattered, but evenly distributed, dimples on the finished product. (This one has been topped with Pecorino Romano cheese.)

Step Seven: Proofing

Proofing is much like bulk fermentation, except by this point the dough has had time to develop and it has been shaped into its final form. Proofing allows the dough to make its final expansion and develop its final structure before baking. It's accomplished by allowing the dough to rest in a pan, couche, or banneton, or on a baking sheet, peel, or work surface before baking. Where it's proofed is largely dependent on how you want the dough to look when it comes out of the oven—this is mainly applicable if it bakes in a pan—and how easy it is to move the dough without damaging it while inserting it into the oven when baking. If it's going to be tough to move the dough without damaging it, then proof it on a baking sheet or peel so that you can easily slip it into the oven. If not, then the work surface will do just fine.

> The higher the hydration level of the dough, the more it will spread out during proofing if it is not proofed in a *banneton*, bowl, or *couche*. Keep this in mind when you're deciding on what you want the final product to look like.

The temperature and humidity considerations for proofing are the same as for bulk fermentation. The choices of what to cover your dough with are the same as what were discussed in the bench rest section above. Here, the main two things to consider are duration of the proofing and timing your proofing in relation to baking.

DURATION

The duration of proofing your dough is wholly dependent upon the dough and the recipe. Recipes generally provide you with a time estimate of how long you should allow the dough to proof. However, time can fluctuate rather drastically, depending on the climate in which you are baking. Altitude and temperature will have the most significant impact on the final rise. Regarding temperature, the general rule is that the warmer your kitchen, the shorter the proofing time, and the cooler your kitchen, the longer it will take. How long it takes depends on your precise location. It can fluctuate by as much as 30%–50% if you are working in an area that is more than 10 to 15 degrees lower or higher than the 75–85°F range recommended for proofing.

The time fluctuation applies to changes in altitude, but with a twist. When baking near sea level, the duration of the proofing will not deviate as much from the suggested proofing time even with a 10- to 15-degree difference in proofing temperature. However, as altitude increases, the proofing will take substantially less time to complete. I've found that baking at an altitude of approximately 6,400 feet reduces the proofing time by as much as 50 percent.

Because of this, you need to be keenly aware of your environment.

> Raise the dough to the degree stated in the recipe (i.e., until it doubles, springs back fully to the touch, springs back partly to the touch, etc.). However, you do not want to overraise the dough (and the directions in the recipe should account for this). You want to hold the dough back just a little bit so that it can make its final rise in the oven for the best final product.

The point to remember here is that you do not want to overproof the dough. Overproofing the dough will cause the internal structure to collapse, which means that the dough will turn out flat—and I do mean flat—and it will be virtually inedible. And into the trash it will go.

> This is one stage where developing a sixth sense for how the dough is developing will help you advance a long way toward producing an award winning loaf of bread.

The main way to determine when the dough has proofed to the proper extent is by feeling it. Gently push a finger against the surface of the dough. If the dough compresses and slowly springs back to its position prior to pushing on it, then the dough has proofed and is ready for baking. If you push on the dough and it remains compressed, it means that you need to give it more time. However, keep in mind that certain dough will deviate from this general rule, so be on the lookout for any nuances in what level the dough should be proofed to.

> The look and feel of the dough during proofing always trumps what the clock tells you—always!

Ultimately, proper proofing depends on diligence—paying close attention to what you are doing and what you are trying to accomplish—and patience, being open to waiting it out, even if the clock tells you otherwise, to achieve the best result from your efforts. The latter of the two just might be the most difficult to master because, at least in the beginning, you will be treading that fine line between perfect proofing and overproofing. But there is a fallback provision when it comes to proofing that will help you make it through this part of the baking process without ruining your dough. Here it is: It is always better to underproof than overproof. Period. So if you are skittish about allowing the second hand to keep spinning away while your dough ekes its way toward perfection, then hold off on that loaf. Then on the next one, allow the time to increase just a bit and continue down that road until you find the perfect balance. This really is one area where experience pays off, but with the help of the underproofing rule, you can obtain that experience all the sooner without experiencing disastrous results.

TIMING

When I say timing, I mean calculating the time it takes for your dough to achieve its optimal proofing state in relation to the time it takes to preheat your oven for baking. If you are using your oven as your proofing cabinet, then this is much more of a concern, because you will have to remove your dough from the oven long enough in advance for the oven to heat to the baking temperature at the same time your dough is ready. This is a very tricky thing to do because it depends on how long it takes for your oven to heat up and it depends on the ambient air temperature, which will impact

If you are proofing in a *banneton*, dust it with lots of flour to keep the dough from sticking to it. If you use a linen-lined *banneton* for proofing, or a bowl you've lined with a towel, use even more generous amounts of flour to prevent the dough from sticking to the cloth.

your proofing. Regarding the latter, this means that if you have your dough in a comfy 80°F in the oven and then pull it out to a 65°F room temperature, you're going to have some timing issues. At the longest, I recommend that you only allow your dough to proof in the oven for about 50 percent of the proofing time. This should give you enough time to heat your oven and complete the proofing process.

However, the better way of doing this is to proof your dough out of the oven. This way you can begin heating your oven when you begin proofing. This will ensure that your oven is at the proper temperature (and your baking stone is as hot as the oven) and ready to go when the dough is fully proofed. This will also take some of the pressure off of the timing issue.

If you are going to proof on a baking sheet or baker's peel—i.e., something other than what you are going to bake on—then be sure to sprinkle ample amounts of cornmeal on the surface before you place the dough on it. This will help to prevent the dough from sticking to the surface, and if you're going to slide the dough onto your baking stone, it will allow the dough to slide freely into the oven.

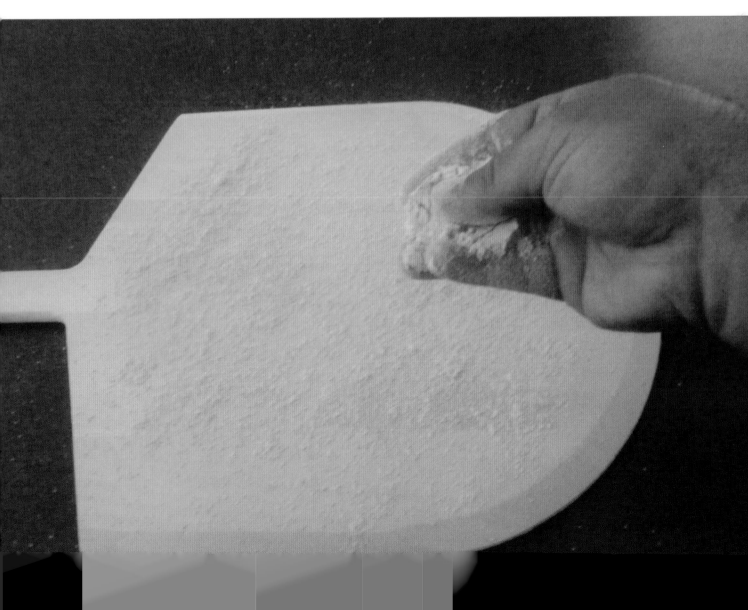

Step Eight: Baking and Cooling

You're in the home stretch now, but don't think for one second that it gets easier from here. As with any of the other steps in the bread-baking process, if you don't accurately carry out the baking procedures listed below, you're not going to obtain the results you'd like. The good news is that it's not that hard to master the baking; all you have to do is follow the rules. If you do that and you've been diligent in performing all of the other steps up to this point, I guarantee that you're going to have a wonderful loaf of bread come out of the oven. But before you get there, you need to take care of a few other matters first.

> Before you even think about baking, make sure that you have tested the temperature of your oven using an oven thermometer to make sure that the temperature reading on the oven itself is actually the temperature you require.

SCORING

Scoring, or slashing, the top of the dough is critical to the success of the baking endeavor. Scoring dough accomplishes two things: First, it allows the dough to expand during the early stages of baking which, in turn, will give the final loaf of bread the perfect internal volume (this is where all of your hard work during the kneading process of building up the internal structure of the dough really pays off). And second, scoring serves as the baker's signature, her stylistic mark on the bread. Although the baker still has to abide by certain rules in the scoring process, there is still enough room for an artistic touch to be imparted to each loaf. In fact, bakers can easily tell which baker scored which loaf of dough in a bakery, all because of the each baker's particular method. Although you'll eventually develop a style of your own, it's much more important for you to score the dough correctly so that the final product comes out tasting delicious, not just looking good. Because of these two sides of the equations, it's easy to see how scoring can be considered both an art and a science.

> Scoring creates an intentional weak spot in the dough so that the dough shapes up the way you want it to. If you didn't score the dough, the surface would rip randomly, thus impacting the quality of the final product.

To begin, you have three options in regard to devices you can use to score dough: a

The initial expansion of the dough in the oven is called oven spring. This is a period of intense fermentation that creates increased gas production, and therefore volume in the loaf. From a technical perspective, yeast remains active until it reaches 140°F. As long as the yeast remains alive, it contributes to the expansion of the dough. However, once the yeast reaches 140°F and it dies, expansion of the dough ceases. This normally occurs within the first third of the baking time.

lame, razor, or knife. The *lame*, which was covered under equipment portion of Section 1, is the tool of choice among bakers. Its handle allows you to see what you are doing, rather than working right on top of the dough. The razor all by itself is the choice of some because it allows you to work closer to the dough. And the knife is most often the last choice, mainly because the *lame* and razor work so well. But the benefit of the knife is that everyone has one in her kitchen. Just make sure that if you use a knife, it's as sharp as you can get it. That will go a long way toward the knife not sticking to the dough. And although a high-quality stainless steel *lame* like many bakers use are not readily available at your local grocery store (I'll tell you where to purchase one in the reference guide at the end of the book.),

a double-edged razor can be found at virtually every drugstore. For that reason, if you can't get your hands on a *lame,* then pick up a pack of razors and use those.

Once you've got your tool, it's time to plan how you are going to score the dough. Certain dough, such as that shaped into a baguette, require a very particular type of score while other dough, such as your run-of-the-mill *boule*, provide for a greater degree of latitude in how you will score it. For example, some *boule*s are scored with a long arc across the center of the dough while others are scored with a box, crisscross, or even a leaf pattern. For dough that require a particular scoring pattern, like the baguette, follow it precisely. It's been developed over the course of centuries, and it works. But for those types of dough that provide you with a bit more creative input, feel free to experiment so long as you incorporate the proper technique into your score.

Before scoring the dough, place it on the piece of equipment—a peel or piece of cardboard—that you will use to transfer the dough to the oven. This way you won't damage the dough while transferring it to the oven.

Here's how to score:

1. Place the dough in front of you and hold the *lame* (or whatever tool you're using

to score with) slightly above, and in front of, the point on the dough where you want to begin slicing. The edge of the blade should be angled toward the dough for an angular cut and straight up and down for a straight cut (depending on which you'd like to incorporate).

Then, with a swift but controlled motion, slice the blade into the dough at the required depth.

2. Continue the scoring motion until the blade has completely exited the dough.
3. Repeat steps 1 and 2 for any additional scores.

The same process on a *batard*.

In general, the blade should be held at 30 to 45 degree angle to the dough for the creation of a flap or "ear" on the final product (baguettes, most notably) to as much as 90 degrees (vertical) for maximum expansion on stronger dough, like sourdough and some Italian and French *boules* and *batards*. Also, the blade should penetrate the dough from ¼ to ½ inch, depending on the strength of the dough (i.e., the stronger the dough, the deeper the cut).

TIPS FOR SCORING

- Before scoring the dough, visually determine where you want each slice to start and end up. Planning ahead will help you to create even scores.
- Hold the *lame* (or other scoring tool) lightly, but firmly. Holding it too tightly or too loosely will likely create an uneven score. You'll get the feel for this after just a few slices.
- The key to scoring dough is to use your entire arm to move the blade, not just your fingers or wrist. This provides for a more uniform slice across the dough.
- The motion of slicing is also deliberate, meaning that you don't drag the blade through the dough, nor do you race it through the dough. A swift but controlled motion works best. At first, the control will likely be missing from your scoring, but

after a few slices, it will feel much more natural.
- Score dough from same side as your body; don't reach over dough.
- For baguettes and other dough on which you'd like to create ears, make sure the blade is curved on your *lame* and that your palm is facing down and the concave side of the blade is facing up.
- For dough in which you want to create a score other than a flap, make sure that the blade on the *lame* is straight.
- By starting the motion of the score in front of the point where you intend to begin slicing helps to make the scoring motion smoother. It will also help to make the slice even in depth and angle right from the beginning of the score. And when you approach the end of the score, follow through with the blade, allowing it to continue cutting into the air once the score is complete. This will help to guarantee that the end of your score is the same as the beginning of your score.
- Make sure you maintain the same blade angle, depth, and pressure over the course of the entire score. If you don't, the dough will not expand uniformly.
- The more you score, the better at it you will become. It's definitely one area of bread baking where repetition pays off.

HOW TO SCORE A BAGUETTE

As stated above, there's quite a bit of liberty on how to score most *batards* and *boules*, but when it comes to baguettes, it's a whole different story. Let's get right to it.

The baguette requires 4 to 6 scores—the longer the loaf the more scores required—that should be contained wholly within the middle third of the top of the dough. The slices must overlap the preceding score about 20–30 percent, be cut at approximately a 30-degree angle to the dough, and be even in length. Because the area in which the scoring will take place on a baguette is so long, it's essential that you visually plan your slices before making them.

The baguette, quite possibly more than any other dough, requires precise scoring in order for it to come out of the oven

Close-up of ear.

Properly scored baguettes.

The final product.

properly expanded. Because of this, pay close attention to what you're doing. Your taste buds will appreciate the extra effort down the road.

Some bakers dust the surface of the dough with either bread or rice flour before scoring, the dough. After scoring, the flour exists only on the nonscored part of the dough, leaving the sliced area to expand without flour on it. This makes for a dramatic contrasting effect when the loaf comes out of the oven.

PREPARING THE OVEN

The focus of preparing the oven is on preheating. In order for the dough to transform into the loaf that you envisioned from the start, the oven must, and I do mean must, be at the proper temperature when the dough is placed in it. As stated earlier, you need to make sure that your oven temperature is accurate, so be sure to test it before you decide to bake bread. You'd be surprised how often ovens signal that the oven has been preheated to the proper temperature, only to find that the thermometer you placed in the oven reads 50 to 100°F less. This is one time when you don't want to take chances. Your final loaf

Master bakers test their apprentices by making the apprentice hold the baguette up by its ear. If the apprentice can do it and the ear doesn't break, she passes. If not, back to the scoring board she goes.

will suffer greatly if baked in an oven that's the wrong temperature.

If possible, always bake your bread on the center shelf of the oven, which will help the dough to bake uniformly. And if you see that your dough is becoming more browned on one side when compared to the others, rotate the dough in the oven to make sure it bakes evenly. Many ovens, both home and commercial, have natural hot spots (i.e., places that are hotter than others and bake more quickly). Although you'll never get rid of them, if you know where they are, you'll be able to manipulate your oven accordingly for proper baking.

But it's not just important to preheat your oven. There are two other essential pieces of equipment that require preheating: the baking stone and the sheet pan used for steaming. I cannot stress the importance of preheating your baking stone if you are using one. Think of it this way, your oven may be at 475°F, but if your stone has not yet reached 475°F and you place your dough upon it, you have just undermined your efforts because the dough will drop to the temperature of the stone. The lower temperature will produce a less than perfect result.

Baking stones, particularly those ¾ inch or greater in thickness, can take an hour or more to preheat, so be sure to factor this into your time calculations.

In addition to the baking stone, it's very helpful to preheat the sheet pan that you will use for creating steam (which will be discussed next). If you do not preheat the sheet pan, then steam production will be less than what is desired. The best way to preheat the sheet pan is to place it in the oven along with the baking stone when you turn the oven on. That way, your sheet pan will be hot, and your oven components will be ready when the dough informs you that it's time to bake it.

You'll find that the majority of dough is baked at one of two temperatures: lean dough (dough that doesn't incorporate fat) is most often baked in the 460–500°F range while enriched dough is baked in the 350–375°F range. If you can remember those figures, you'll be able to determine right from the start when you need to start preheating your oven. And when you find recipes that might not have been created by professionals, you'll also be able to tell if you need to tweak the temperature at which you bake the bread.

A properly set up oven with baking stone and sheet pan in place.

GETTING THE DOUGH IN THE OVEN

Now you have to get the dough in the oven. For the most part it's an easy task, but there are a few tips that will help you get the job done that much easier and, more important, without damaging your dough. Here I'll focus on how to use a peel and a flipping board (or a piece of stiff cardboard instead).

A peel is used as follows:

1. Place your dough on the surface of the well-floured (or cornmealed) peel (here, a piece of cardboard for demonstration), with the front edge of the dough at the front edge of the peel. Then insert your peel into the oven so that the front edge of the peel is closer to the back end of the baking stone. Tilt the peel downward toward the baking stone so that the front edge of the peel is touching the surface of the baking stone.

2. Using short, quick jerks, pull the peel away from the oven. With the cornmeal or flour acting as a lubricant, the dough will slide off the peel and onto the baking stone.

If you intend to bake your dough on a clay or ceramic baking sheet, make sure that you preheat the baking sheet before placing the dough on it. If you don't preheat it, the clay or ceramic will be cold and will slow down the baking process. This will prevent the dough from heating properly during the initial stages of baking and will negatively impact both the bottom of the dough and the crumb.

The above technique works well for *boules* and *batards*, which can be moved much more easily from the proofing surface to the peel without damaging the dough. However, with more delicate dough shapes, such as the baguette, you'll need to be a little more careful. The best way to transfer a baguette from the *couche* to the oven is with the help of the flipping board.

The same technique is demonstrated with a wood peel and a *boule*.

Here's how to use one:

1. Place a flipping board doused dusted with flour or cornmeal directly adjacent to the dough in the *couche*.
2. Lift the edge of the *couche* up so that the dough begins to roll toward the flipping board.

3. Continue lifting the *couche* and rolling the dough until it rolls onto the flipping board. Be deliberate in this final motion, but don't crush the dough in the process. Once the dough is on the flipping board, use it just like a peel.

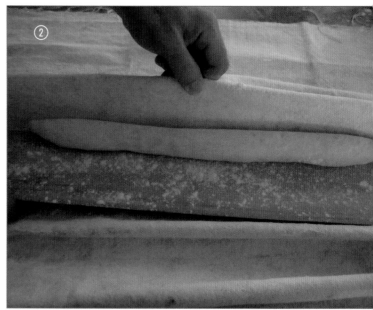

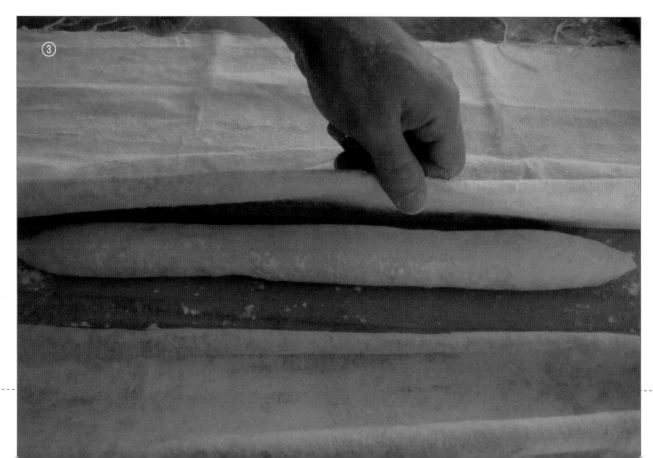

That's about all there is to it. One piece of advice, though: Make sure you maintain control over your peel, flipping board, or cardboard and the dough resting upon it because you don't want to be too forceful in your movements and scoot the dough off the back or sides of the baking stone. Other than that, it's time to move on to steaming and venting.

STEAMING AND VENTING

Steaming is the secret of the pros, at least as far as obtaining a crispy crust goes. By adding steam to the oven, moisture adheres to the surface of the dough. The moisture is a perfect heat conductor, so the surface of the dough attracts more heat than if it were not steamed. The moisture, along with the added heat, causes the surface of the dough to brown. When the surface of the dough caramelizes, it becomes crusty. And when it becomes crusty, you've made it to the big leagues!

Remember, steaming has its greatest effect during the first 1/3 of baking time.

Creating steam in the oven is simple, but it's not just about adding water to the oven. No, there's a method for doing so that will produce the best results.

Commercial bakeries use steam-injected ovens that inject steam directly into the oven as the dough bakes. The baker can precisely control the amount of steam that is released into the oven to obtain the exact result she is looking for. Because these ovens can cost tens and tens of thousands of dollars, the home baker has to manually introduce steam into the oven. You'll never be able to get the same result as the expensive commercial ovens, but you'll be able to come close.

To create steam in your oven, you will need a large sheet pan, some water, and preferably a spray bottle filled with water. The reason for using a large baking sheet is all about creating increased amounts of steam. Home ovens are designed to rid the oven of moisture, so the oven will do everything in its power to expel the precious steam from its confines. To account for the forced steam expulsion caused by your oven, you have to introduce quite a bit of steam in the beginning to compensate for this. Using a large sheet pan is the best way to combat this problem because the larger surface area of the sheet pan will create more steam than a smaller surface area when you pour water onto its preheated surface.

To steam the oven:

1. Place a towel over the oven window (to prevent water from landing on it and causing it to crack) and pour boiling water onto the sheet pan that's on the bottom shelf in the oven.

2. Then using the spray bottle, squirt the lower sides of the oven 8 to 10 times. Remove the towel from the oven window and quickly close the oven door.

TIPS FOR STEAMING

- Have your water, spray bottle, and towel ready to go when you intend to steam. If you have to look around for these items when the oven door is open, you're going to lose precious heat.
- Do not spray water directly onto the baking stone. The temperature shock can cause the stone to warp or crack.
- Because it's difficult to create steam at home as well as one could in a

Steam Safety: The initial burst of steam in the oven can cause serious burns, so keep your face and hands as far away from the steam as possible. To combat this, use a watering can with a long neck, if you can find one, to pour water into your sheet pan when steaming. This will help to prevent steam burns by increasing the distance between the steam and your hands and face. It also helps to use a towel to hold the container you're pouring water with to avoid burning your hand.

commercial bakery, it's acceptable to lightly mist the top of dough with the sprayer before inserting the dough into the oven to help increase moisture on both the surface of the dough and in the oven. However, indirect steam seems to work so much better, so avoid misting the dough unless you just can't seem to create enough steam as described.

Naturally leavened bread like sourdough takes longer to achieve optimal oven spring, so steam the oven again 1 to 2 minutes after initial steaming.

VENTING

Allowing the steam to remain in the oven for the entire baking process will prevent the development of a nice crust. Because of this, you will need to vent the oven, or allow the steam to escape, during the final 10 minutes of baking.

To vent the dough, open the oven door to just enough to insert something—I prefer a pair of steel tongs—to keep the door cracked open. This will allow the steam to continue to escape while still allowing the dough to bake. Then allow the dough to continuing baking for the prescribed amount of time—or, more accurately until the time that you feel the dough is ready to leave the oven.

As with steaming, be sure to keep your face clear of the venting steam to avoid being burned. And use a towel as well when you're propping the oven door open. Safety is of paramount importance in the kitchen.

Venting with tongs.

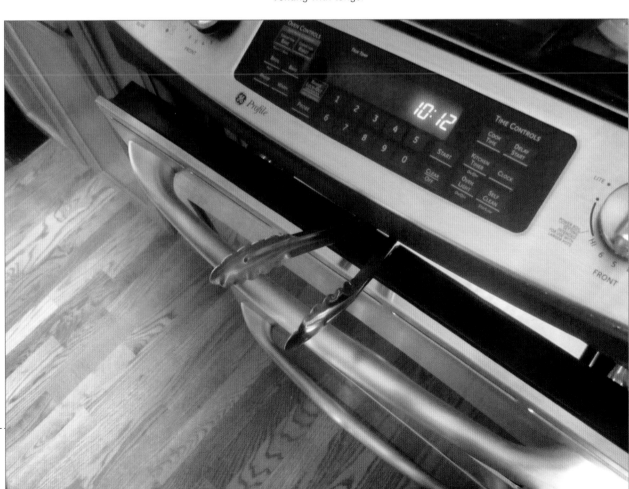

BAKING

After making all of the initial preparations above, your focus should now be on the duration of baking. Recipes will give you an estimate of how long the dough will need to remain in the oven, but remember that these are not exact figures. As you've most certainly realized by now, there are many factors that play into how long your dough will actually spend in the oven. However, as discussed in relation to bulk fermentation and proofing, altitude may be the most significant factor.

> Never, and I mean never, tell anyone that you are going to cook your bread. You bake bread, not cook it. And you call the session of baking a "bake," as in, "I had a good bake today." That's all there is to it when it comes to talking like the pros.

Dough bakes faster as altitude increases. In fact, when I've baked at an altitude of 6,400 feet, my baking times have decreased by as much as 40 percent when compared to baking at sea level. If you're baking at elevations of under several thousand feet, this should not be much of a concern, but if you're approaching 5,000 or more feet, then you definitely have to be cognizant of this fact, more so with lean dough rather than enriched dough. And mastering this really comes down to one thing: paying attention to what your dough is doing in the oven.

> The reason you'll see some artisan breads with very dark crusts is because certain breads, particularly some varieties of sourdough, require longer baking in order to obtain a crunchy crust.

This task is much easier if your oven has a window. That way you can get a pretty good look at what the dough is doing. But even so, at some point you're going to have to open the oven door and take a look since looking through the oven window doesn't exactly provide you with the clearest look of what's going on inside. If you have to open the door to see what's going on, because you either don't have a window or can't see well enough through the window, do not open the door until the initial steaming process has advanced through its course. This means that you should probably wait 10 to 20 minutes before opening the door. The time will depend wholly on the length of baking. But once the initial steaming period is complete, it's a perfect time to look inside to see how your dough is shaping up.

At this point, look for evenness of baking. The main thing to look for is whether one side of the dough is darker than another. If not, leave it alone. If it is, then rotate the dough in the oven so that the lighter side is now where the darker side was. And at this point, the dough has baked long enough so that rotating it in the oven should be easy in that the dough won't stick to the baking stone.

At this juncture, it's also important to discuss conventional versus convection baking. Conventional baking is when you simply turn the oven on to a temperature, and the dough bakes at that temperature. Convection baking uses the help of a fan in the oven to circulate the hot air in the oven, which in theory creates a more even baking environment. However, the major problem with convection baking in the home oven is that the side of the dough closest to the fan inherently receives a greater amount of heat because the fan is forcing the hot air onto that side of the dough. Ironically, this results in greater inconsistency in bread baking at home (although for other types of baking, it can be a godsend). For this reason, it's best to use conventional baking for bread at home. However, if you are determined to use a convection oven, remember to lower the temperature by about 25 degrees, rotate the dough during baking to avoid overbaking one side, and reduce the baking time since the convection causes quicker baking for the most part.

After taking all of this into consideration, the next question is, How do you know when the bread is done baking? Once again, making this determination is a science and an art. From the scientific perspective, lean dough is generally finished baking when its internal temperature reaches 200–205°F, although *ciabatta* can reach 210°F while enriched dough is fully baked at an internal temperature of 185–190°F. If you want to test your bread this way, insert a chef's thermometer into the bread so that the tip of the thermometer is in the center of the loaf. Leave it there for 5 to 10 seconds and take the temperature.

The temperature of baked bread drops rather quickly after removing it from the oven, so if you're taking its internal temperature, do so as soon as you pull it from the oven to obtain the most accurate reading for doneness.

Although the above method is accurate, there's something just plain wrong about using a thermometer to tell when your bread is done baking. It takes the fun out of it. Instead, there are more practical ways to tell. The first is to look at the bread. Does the crust look like its browning to the proper degree? If not, leave it in the oven. If it is, then remove the bread from the oven and thump your fingers on the bottom of the

bread. If it sounds hollow, it's done. If not, put it back in the oven. Another way that bakers tell when lean dough is fully baked is to listen to it. That's right. Place your ear up close to the crust and listen to your bread. If it's fully baked, you'll hear it crackle. But even with these techniques, it still comes down to getting a feel for when the bread is done baking. As the Central Intelligence Agency directs its operatives, go with your gut; it never lies, so too does the master baker to her apprentice. That said, in the beginning, rely upon the suggested baking times in the recipe; just keep in mind the caveat about altitude.

COOLING

If you're dying to bite into that bread as soon as it comes out of the oven, don't do it. Of course I know you're going to disregard that direct order when you first start out— hell, I did!—but once you understand why it's better to wait, then your patience levels will increase dramatically. For now, just place the bread on a cooling rack and be patient.

The question is, How long do you leave it there before cutting into the loaf? Ideally, two to three hours. This will allow plenty of time for the bread to cool thoroughly so that its qualities shine through when you taste it. But cooling duration will be impacted by the temperature and draftiness of your cooling environment. So keep that in mind as well.

The reason for taking your time at this stage is that the full flavor of the bread will not penetrate your taste buds at a higher temperature. Sure, there will be a flavor, but it will not be as strong as if you were to let the bread cool properly. Also, if you cut into the bread while it is too hot, you will no doubt crush the crumb that you just spent hours creating. You'll end up tasting a glueyer crumb than the bread is capable of putting forth if it is cooled to the proper degree.

The moral of the story is, Wait! It's worth it.

STORAGE

I can't discuss baking and cooling bread without also discussing how to store it, for what good is the bread if it's only good to eat for an hour or two? There are a multitude of factors that weigh into how long your bread will last, including, most significantly, temperature and humidity. In general, however, bread created from straight dough will last a much shorter time than will bread created from created from enriched dough, prefermented dough, or sourdough. The fat content and the prefermented element of these types of bread act as natural preservatives.

But beyond that generalization, professionals recommend storing your bread at room temperature rather than in the refrigerator. In the longer term, you can

Place your bread on end when it's on the cutting board to prevent the crumb from drying out.

store bread in the freezer. However, the same rules apply: prefermented and enriched bread will retain more of their natural qualities longer than bread made from straight dough.

I've found that storing bread in an airtight container or in a plastic bag works well in the short term since it keeps the bread moist. But try to use the bread quickly because if you leave it in such a container or bag for more than a few days, the trapped moisture becomes a wonderful breeding ground for mold.

Bringing bread back to life can be accomplished in the oven. If the crumb is still nice but the crust is a little soft, place the bread in a 400°F oven for a few minutes until the crust crisps up again. If you need to spruce up the entire loaf, place it in a 350°F oven for 5 to 10 minutes. But remember, the more you attempt to revive the bread, the quicker it will stale.

And guess what: You've made it! You now understand the ingredients, equipment, and techniques involved in baking bread. There's only one thing left to do: bake. Let's jump in to tackling some classic recipes in the next section.

Recipes

IN THIS SECTION, I'VE INCLUDED RECIPES FOR straight, prefermented, and enriched dough, as well as sourdough. These recipes will incorporate all that you've learned this far, and you'll also discover additional techniques and tips that will help you craft each particular type of bread. And by the time you've finished baking all these, you'll have all the skills and experience you need to elevate your bread baking to a higher level and bake pretty much any type of bread you desire.

Before you begin working on any of these recipes, calculate the overall time it will take to complete each step and the overall process. This will set you up for success right from the start—both mentally and physically.

I've provided the baker's percentages for all the recipes. The baker's percentage is fully described at the end of the chapter. Placing it right in front would likely cause confusion—it sure did for me—but I assure you that it will make much more sense when you've looked through the recipes.

Straight Dough

As you've already learned, straight dough is dough in which all ingredients are mixed at once. These are great for when you'd like a fresh loaf of bread but didn't plan ahead. Sure, the flavor isn't as fully developed as the prefermented breads and sourdough, but after all, fresh bread is better than no bread at all. Here are two recipes: one for white wheat and one for whole wheat bread. Each will make about 908 grams (2 pounds) of dough. These are great to start with because you don't have to mess with a preferment; you can bake them whenever you want, and the hydration level is on the lower side, which a great place to start to work your way into the wetter dough to come.

White—DDT: 78°F

Ingredient	Weight	Baker's Percentage
Bread Flour	567 grams	100%
Yeast	5 grams	1%
Water	385 grams	68%
Salt	14 grams	2.4%

Whole Wheat—DDT: 78°F

Ingredient	Weight	Baker's Percentage
Bread Flour	340 grams	60%
Whole Wheat Flour	227 grams	40%
Yeast	5 grams	1%
Water	397 grams	70%
Salt	14 grams	2.4%

Note: The whole wheat flour requires more water than white wheat in order to create a more appealing crumb.

1. Select which recipe from above that you are going to use.

2. Mix the ingredients according to the instructions in the "Mixing" portion of section 2 (pages 43–44).

3. Knead according to the instruction contained in the "Kneading" portion of section 2 (pages 48–49). Because this dough has a relatively low hydration, I recommend using the conventional kneading technique, although you may need to use the French method a few times just to get the dough into a more workable consistency. Knead until the gluten has fully developed and the dough can pass the window test. Note: The whole wheat dough recipe will never pass the window test because the hulls in the flour cut the gluten strands. Just make sure that the dough is nice and elastic before moving on to the next step. This may take from 10 to 15 minutes of kneading depending on how fast and deliberate you are. (One side effect of kneading is that you get a workout in, too!)

4. Bulk ferment the dough according to the instructions in "Bulk Fermentation" portion of section 2 (page 59). Bulk ferment for 30–45 minutes, or until the dough has just about doubled; fold the dough using one of the two techniques described in the "Bulk Fermentation" section, then ferment for an additional 30 minutes. Fold again and ferment for another 15 minutes. Note: For the whole wheat dough, use the second folding technique. It will work much better due to the stiffer nature of the dough.

5. Following the instructions set forth in the "Preshaping" portion of section 2 (pages 76–79), shape the dough into an oblong (if you'd like the final shape to be a *batard*) or a round (if you'd like the final shape to be a *boule*). Remember, you can always make smaller loaves or rolls as well. Just divide the dough accordingly (i.e., in half for one-pound loaves and into 60 gram pieces for rolls).

6. After preshaping, let the dough rest for 15–20 minutes.

7. Using the instructions outlined in the "Final Shaping" portion of section 2 (pages 83–91), form your dough into its final shape.

8. Proof the dough according to the instructions set forth in the "Proofing" portion of section 2 (pages 108–112). The dough should be covered, and proofing should take approximately 45–60 minutes, or until the dough springs back to the touch. If the dough remains dented after touching, continue proofing the dough until it springs back. (A perfect example where patience pays off!)

9. Score the dough according to the instructions set forth in the "Scoring" portion of section 2 (pages 113–114).

10. Place your dough in the oven and steam the oven according to the instructions set forth in the "Baking" portion of section 2 (page 126).

11. Bake the dough at 460°F for approximately 25–30 minutes (but

remember, this may change depending on altitude and your oven). Remember to vent the oven during the final 10 minutes of baking. Test for doneness by using a thermometer or thumping the bottom of the loaf. You can also listen for that crackling sound if you place it close to your ear. The crust should be golden brown.

12. Cool the bread according to the instructions set forth in the "Cooling" portion of section 2 (pages 130–131).

13. Congratulations! You've baked your first loaf!

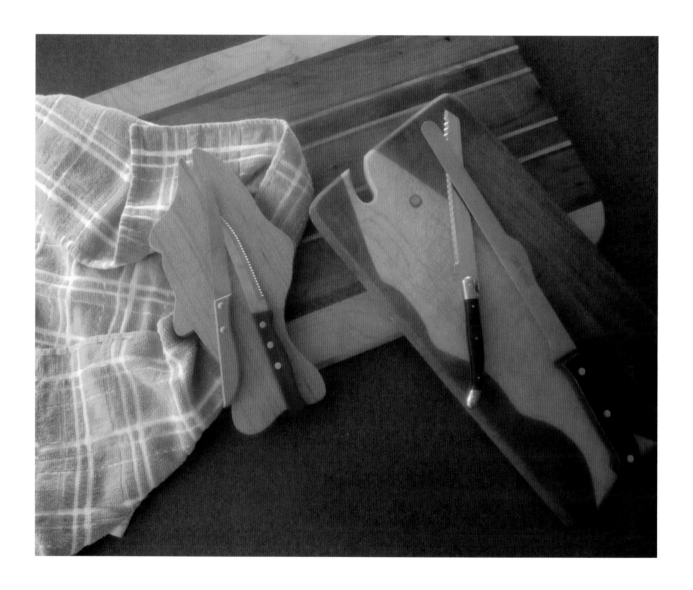

Prefermented

Once you've tackled straight dough, and you've loved the taste and texture of the bread, you're no doubt going to want to dive into the prefermented dough. This is where the real magic begins. In addition to adding a wonderful flavor dimension to the dough, their increased acidity levels strengthen the gluten and act as a natural preservative, thus extending the life of the bread well beyond straight dough.

Prefermented dough comes in three varieties: *biga*, *poolish*, or *pâte fermentée*. *Biga* is the Italian version of a preferment and is composed of a ratio of 50–60 percent water weight to 100 percent flour weight, along with a small amount of yeast. It typically ferments from anywhere from 8–24 hours. A *poolish* is a French version (actually it was brought to France by the Polish by way of Vienna, hence the name) of a preferment. It consists of equal weights of water and flour, along with a small amount of yeast. The *poolish* is typically fermented for

12–15 hours. This preferment is the heart and soul of baguettes. And last, but not least, is *pâte fermentée*, which means "old dough" in French. It's nothing more than a piece of dough leftover from another recipe that has been allowed to ferment in the refrigerator. To incorporate this preferment, add a ratio of about 30 percent *pâte fermentée* by weight (or a little more or less if it better suits your taste) to 100 percent flour weight to one of the straight dough recipes. This is a great way to add some flavor to a recipe if you've thought ahead—which I just can't ever seem to remember to do—and reserved from dough from a prior recipe.

Smell your preferments once they've fully developed. It will give you a good idea of the flavor that will be imparted to the final product.

Biga just after mixing and twenty-four hours later.

Poolish just after mixing and fifteen hours later.

Enough explanation. It's time to put some bread on the table.

By French law, baguettes can be made using only flour, water, yeast, and salt. Adding any other ingredient to the dough precludes it from being a baguette. So keep that in mind when you're looking at variations on baguette recipes. For me, this is also in part how I judge the authenticity of a baking recipe book. If I see a recipe that calls for malt powder or butter or some other ingredient in a baguette, I immediately put it down and look elsewhere. Call it harsh, but a baguette is a baguette.

BAGUETTE DOUGH WITH POOLISH

Although this type of dough is commonly called baguette dough and is shaped in the form of baguettes, feel free to use the *batard* and *boule* shapes as well.

Poolish—DDT: 78°F

Makes enough dough for about 908 grams (2 pounds) of bread

Ingredient	Weight	Baker's Percentage of Poolish
Bread Flour	170 grams	100%
Water	170 grams	100%
Yeast	A pinch	About .04%

Dough

Ingredient	Weight	Baker's Percentage of Final Dough
Bread Flour	450 grams	72.5%
Yeast	5 grams	.08%
Water	295 grams	47.5%
Poolish	340 grams	54.8%
Salt	15 grams	2.5%

1. To form the *poolish*, add the flour and yeast to 60°F water. Mix until thoroughly combined—it will have the feel of a medium-thick batter—then place the *poolish* in a container, cover, and allow it to ferment 75°F for 14–15 hours. (I suggest starting with 15 and working backward—but to no less than 12 hours—if you feel the flavor is too strong).

2. After your *poolish* is ready, mix the ingredients, including the *poolish*, according to the instructions in the "Mixing" portion of section 2 (pages 43–44). Remember, because we're using a preferment, the water, *poolish*, and salt are combined then the flour and yeast are added.

3. Knead according to the instructions contained in the "Kneading" portion of section 2 (pages 48–52). Because the hydration level of this dough is 75 percent, it will be more wet that with the previous recipes. So, I recommend using the French kneading technique until the dough comes together to the point where it gets tough to stretch and fold the dough during the French kneading process. At that point, switch over to the conventional kneading technique. Knead until the gluten has fully developed and the dough can pass the window test. This may take from 10 to 15 minutes of kneading, depending on how fast and deliberate you are.

4. Bulk ferment the dough according to the instructions in "Bulk Fermentation" portion of section 2 (page 89). Bulk ferment for 45–60 minutes, or until the dough has just about doubled; fold the dough using one of the two techniques described in the "Bulk Fermentation" section then ferment for an additional 30 minutes. Fold again and ferment for another 15 minutes.

5. Following the instructions set forth in the "Preshaping" portion of section 2 (pages 76–79), shape the dough into an oblong for a batard or baguette (300 gram pieces will make 16- to 18-inch-long baguettes), or a round (if you'd like the final shape to be a *batard*), or a round (if you'd like the final shape to be a *boule*). Remember, you can always make smaller loaves or rolls as well. Just divide the dough accordingly (i.e., in half for one-pound loaves and into 60 gram pieces for rolls).

6. After preshaping, let the dough rest for 15–20 minutes.

7. Using the instructions outlined in the "Final Shaping" portion of section 2 (pages 83–91), form your dough into its final shape.

8. Proof the dough according to the instructions set forth in the "Proofing" portion of section 2 (pages 108–112). If you are making baguettes, remember to proof them in a *couche*. The dough should be covered, and proofing should take approximately 30–45 minutes, or until the dough springs back to the touch. If the dough remains dented after lightly touching it, continue proofing the dough until it springs back.

9. Score the dough according to the instructions set forth in the "Scoring" portion of section 2 (pages 113–114).

10. Place your dough in the oven and steam the oven according to the instructions set forth in the "Baking" portion of section 2 (page 126).

11. Bake the dough at 470°F for approximately 20–25 minutes (but remember, this may change, depending on altitude and your oven). Remember to vent the oven during the final 10 minutes of baking. Test for doneness by using a thermometer or thumping the bottom of the loaf. You can also listen for that crackling sound if you place it close to your ear. The crust should be golden brown.

12. Cool the bread according to the instructions set forth in the "Cooling" portion of section 2 (pages 130–131).

Because *biga* is Italian in heritage, any dough that includes a *biga* will produce an Italian-style bread.

LEAN DOUGH WITH BIGA

Biga—DDT: 78°F

Makes enough dough for about 908 grams (2 pounds) of bread

Ingredient	Weight	Baker's Percentage of Biga
Bread Flour	170 grams	100%
Water	94 grams	55%
Yeast	A pinch	about .04%

Dough

Ingredient	Weight	Baker's Percentage of Final Dough
Bread Flour	398 grams	70%
Yeast	4 grams	.07%
Water	295 grams	51.9%
Biga	264 grams	46.4%
Salt	14 grams	2.5%

1. To form the *biga*, add the flour and yeast to 60°F water. Mix until thoroughly combined—you may have to use the

conventional kneading technique to accomplish this—then place in a container, cover, and allow it to ferment at 75°F for 18–24 hours. (I suggest starting with 24 and working backward if you feel the flavor is too strong).

2. After your *biga* is ready, mix the ingredients, including the *biga*, according to the instructions in the "Mixing" portion of section 2 (pages 43–44). Remember, because we're using a preferment, the water, *biga*, and salt are combined then the flour and yeast are added. Note: Because the *biga* is so stiff, allow it to sit in the water for several minutes so it can soften up before adding the flour and yeast.

3. Knead according to the instructions in the "Kneading Instructions" section 2 (pages 48–49). Because this dough has a relatively low hydration, I recommend using the conventional kneading technique. Knead until the gluten has fully developed and the dough can pass the window test. This may take from 10 to 15 minutes of kneading, depending on how fast and deliberate you are.

4. Bulk ferment the dough according to the instructions in Bulk Fermentation portion of section 2 (page 59). Bulk ferment for 45–60 minutes, or until the dough has just about doubled; fold the dough using one of the two techniques described in the "Bulk Fermentation" section then ferment for an additional 30 minutes. Fold again and ferment for another 15 minutes.

5. Following the instructions set forth in the "Preshaping" portion of section 2 (pages 76–79), shape the dough into an oblong (if you'd like the final shape to be a *batard*) or a round (if you'd like the final shape to be a *boule*). Remember, you can always make smaller loaves or rolls as well. Just divide the dough accordingly (i.e., in half for one-pound loaves and into 60 gram pieces for rolls).

6. After preshaping, let the dough rest for 15–20 minutes.

7. Using the instructions outlined in the "Final Shaping" portion of section 2 (pages 83–91), form your dough into its final shape.

8. Proof the dough according to the instructions set forth in the "Proofing" portion of section 2 (pages 108–112). The dough should be covered, and proofing should take approximately 30–45 minutes, or until the dough springs back to the touch. If the dough remains dented after touching, continue proofing the dough until it springs back. (A perfect example where patience pays off!)

9. Score the dough according to the instructions set forth in the "Scoring" portion of section 2 (pages 113–114).

10. Place your dough in the oven and steam the oven according to the instructions set forth in the "Baking" portion of section 2 (page 126).

11. Bake the dough at 460°F for approximately 25–30 minutes (but remember, this may change depending on altitude and your oven). Remember

to vent the oven during the final 10 minutes of baking. Test for doneness by using a thermometer or thumping the bottom of the loaf. You can also listen for that crackling sound if you place it close to your ear. The crust should be golden brown.

12. Cool the bread according to the instructions set forth in the "Cooling" portion of section 2 (pages 130–131).

For a variation, try using an egg white wash on top of dough before baking. This will give the bread a light but crispy crust, one that's a bit different than that achieved through using steam alone.

Biga can sometimes dry out on the surface in less humid climates. If you're finding that this is an issue where you live, try applying a very thin coat of oil on the *biga* right when you place it in the container to develop, or once it's fully developed, place the warm water you're using in your recipe in the container with the *biga* for about 10 minutes before adding the rest of the ingredients. Doing so will allow the skin on the *biga* to soften up so that it can be fully incorporated into the rest of the dough without being lumpy.

There's nothing that says you can't use your imagination when shaping dough.

> Lean dough with biga is perfect for making pizza. When you arrive at the baking stage, just shape it like a pizza, add your favorite toppings, and bake (no need for steaming).

CIABATTA

Biga– DDT: 78°F

Makes enough dough for about 1,021 grams (2.25 pounds) of bread

Ingredient	Weight	Baker's Percentage of Biga
Bread Flour	184 grams	100%
Water	92 grams	50%
Yeast	A pinch	about .04%

Dough

Ingredient	Weight	Baker's Percentage of Final Dough
Bread Flour	380 grams	67.3%
Yeast	2 grams	.04%
Water	321 grams	56.9%
Biga	276 grams	48.9%
Salt	14 grams	2.5%

1. To form the *biga*, add the flour and yeast to 60°F water. Mix until thoroughly combined—you may have to use the conventional kneading technique to accomplish this—then place in a container, cover, and allow it to ferment at 75°F for 18–24 hours. (I suggest starting with 24 and working backward if you feel the flavor is too strong).

2. After your *biga* is ready, mix the ingredients, including the biga, according to the instructions in the "Mixing" portion of section 2 (pages 43–44). Remember, because we're using a preferment, the water, *biga*, and salt are combined then the flour and yeast are added. Note: Because the *biga* is so stiff, allow it to sit in the water for several minutes so it can soften up before adding the flour and yeast.

3. Knead according to the instructions in the "Kneading Instructions" section 2 (pages 50–52). Because this dough has a high level of hydration, I recommend using the French kneading technique. However, bear in mind that the although the dough will become more smooth, it's never going to come fully together due to its high water content. The key here is to make sure all the ingredients are nicely incorporated. This may take from 10 to 15 minutes of kneading, depending on how fast and deliberate you are.

4. Bulk ferment the dough according to the instructions in Bulk Fermentation portion of section 2 (page 59). Bulk ferment for 30–45 minutes, or until the dough has just about doubled; fold the dough using one of the two techniques described in the

"Bulk Fermentation" section then ferment for an additional 30 minutes. Fold again and ferment for another 15 minutes.

5. *Ciabatta* is not preshaped. Therefore, proceed to the instructions outlined in the "Final Shaping" portion of section 2 (pages 103–105) to form the dough into its final shape.

6. Proof the dough according to the instructions set forth in the "Proofing" portion of section 2 (pages 108–112). Remember to use a *couche* to proof the dough. The dough should be covered, and proofing should take approximately 30–45 minutes, or until the dough springs back to the touch. If the dough remains dented after touching, continue proofing the dough until it springs back. (A perfect example where patience pays off!)

7. *Ciabatta* is not scored, so skip this step.

8. Gently flip the *ciabatta* onto a peel and place your dough in the oven. Steam according to the instructions set forth in the "Baking" portion of section 2 (page 126).

9. Bake the dough at 460°F for approximately 25–30 minutes (but remember, this may change depending on altitude and your oven). Remember to vent the oven during the final 10 minutes of baking. Test for doneness by using a thermometer or thumping the bottom of the loaf. The crust should be golden brown.

10. Cool the bread according to the instructions set forth in the "Cooling" portion of section 2 (pages 130–131).

Ciabatta is very wet, or "slack." In fact, it looks too wet to work with or do anything with once you mix it. But rest assured, after some French knseading and folding, the dough will come together quite nicely in the end.

FOCACCIA

Biga—DDT: 78°F

Makes enough dough for about 908 grams (2 pounds) of bread; will fill an 8 x 12 inch sheet pan

Ingredient	Weight	Baker's Percentage of Biga
Bread Flour	120 grams	100%
Water	66 grams	55%
Yeast	A pinch	about .04%

Dough

Ingredient	Weight	Baker's Percentage of Final Dough
Bread Flour	400 grams	76.9%
Yeast	4 grams	.07%
Water	286 grams	55%
Biga	188 grams	36.1%
Salt	13 grams	2.5%

1. To form the *biga*, add the flour and yeast to 60°F water. Mix until thoroughly

combined—you may have to use the conventional kneading technique to accomplish this—then place in a container, cover, and allow it to ferment at 75°F for 8–12 hours. (I suggest starting with 8 hours and working up if you feel the flavor is too weak).

2. After your *biga* is ready, mix the ingredients, including the *biga*, according to the instructions in the "Mixing" portion of section 2 (pages 43–44). Remember, because we're using a preferment, the water, *biga*, and salt are combined then the flour and yeast are added.

3. Knead according to the instructions in the "Kneading Instructions" section 2 (pages 48–49). Because this dough has a relatively low hydration, I recommend using the conventional kneading technique. Knead until the gluten has fully developed and the dough can pass the window test. This may take from 10 to 15 minutes of kneading, depending on how fast and deliberate you are.

4. Bulk ferment the dough according to the instructions in Bulk Fermentation portion of section 2 (page 59). Bulk ferment for 45–60 minutes, or until the dough has just about doubled; fold the dough using one of the two techniques described in the "Bulk Fermentation" section then ferment for an additional 45 minutes.

5. Following the instructions set forth in the "Preshaping" portion of section 2 (pages 76–77), shape the dough into a round.

6. After preshaping, let the dough rest for 15–20 minutes.

7. Using the instructions outlined in the "Final Shaping" portion of section 2 (pages 105–107), form your dough into its final shape on a sheet pan.

8. Proof the dough according to the instructions set forth in the "Proofing" portion of section 2 (page 106). The dough should be covered, and proofing should take approximately 30–45 minutes, or until the dough springs back to the touch. If the dough remains dented after lightly touching it, continue proofing the dough until it springs back.

9. Brush the dough with olive oil, and dimple the dough with your fingertips as described in the "Final Shaping" portion of section 2 (page 107). If you are going to add any ingredients to the top of the *focaccia*, such as parmesan cheese, salt, onions, or olives—all common toppings, but let your imagination run wild here—do so after brushing with oil and dimpling. (*Focaccia* does not get scored.)

10. Place your dough in the oven and steam the oven according to the instructions set forth in the "Baking" portion of section 2 (page 126).

11. Bake the dough at 460°F for approximately 25–30 minutes (but remember, this may change depending on altitude and your oven). Remember to vent the oven during the final 10 minutes of baking. Test for doneness by using a thermometer or thumping the

bottom of the loaf—although the latter is tough to do because the dough is in a baking sheet. Ultimately, the best indicator is the crust, which should be golden brown.

12. Remove the *focaccia* from the sheet pan, and cool the bread according to the instructions set forth in the "Cooling" portion of section 2 (pages 130–131) .

If you are going to use toppings on the *focaccia*, be sure to prepare them ahead of time so that you're not scrambling to find them when the dough is ready to go in the oven. Translation: Remember your *mise en place!*

If using ingredients, be sure to salt them *and* the top of the *focaccia* before placing it in the oven. This will greatly enhance the flavor of the end product. My preference is kosher salt because it has larger flakes, but ultimately it's a matter of taste.

Enriched Dough

It's now time to talk fat and sugar—two of my best friends in the whole wide world! You will find as many similarities as differences in preparing these types of dough when compared to straight and prefermented dough. However, the texture of the crust and crumb are entirely different, and are a wonder unto themselves—thanks to the help of my buddies, fat and sugar. And I promise that once you master these recipes, you will never again consider buying any of these at a bakery. There's just no comparison when it comes to quality.

Note: Keep in mind that for enriched dough that incorporates a lot of fat—brioche and challah, for example—bulk fermentation will take longer. If you recall the discussion earlier, fat coats the gluten strands, which retards their development (i.e., they don't elongate and become as elastic as quickly as dough that doesn't incorporate fat).

PAIN DE MIE

Pain de mie is the French equivalent of American white bread. I will tell you without hesitation that this is a far superior product to the American

version. I know, I know, that's not very patriotic to say, but this is one case where the truth must triumph.

Aside from that, this loaf can be baked in a 9 inch x 4 inch x 4 inch Pullman pan (if you want it to come out square in shape) or regular 1.5 pound loaf pan (if you like the top of the loaf rounded). Either way tastes great; it's just a matter of preference and whether you have a Pullman pan on hand.

Dough—DDT: 78°F

Makes enough dough for about 681 grams (1.5 pounds) of bread

Ingredient	Weight	Baker's Percentage of Final Dough
Bread Flour	389 grams	100%
Yeast	4 grams	1%
Water	253 grams	65%
Olive Oil	35 grams	9%
Sugar	16 grams	4.1%
Salt	10 grams	2.6%

1. Mix the ingredients according to the instructions in the "Mixing" portion of section 2 (pages 43–44).
2. Knead according to the instructions in the "Kneading Instructions" section 2 (pages 48–49). Because this dough has a relatively low hydration, I recommend using the conventional kneading technique. Knead until the gluten has fully developed and the dough can pass the window test. This may take from 10 to 15 minutes of kneading, depending on how fast and deliberate you are.
3. Bulk ferment the dough according to the instructions in "Bulk Fermentation" portion of section 2 (page 59). Bulk ferment for 45–60 minutes or until the dough has just about doubled.
4. Following the instructions set forth in the Preshaping portion of section 2 (pages 78–79), shape the dough into an oblong.
5. After preshaping, let the dough rest for 15–20 minutes.
6. Using the instructions outlined in the "Final Shaping" portion of section 2 (pages 83–91), form your dough into its final loaf shape and place the dough in either a well-oiled Pullman pan or a well-oiled 1.5 pound loaf pan.
7. Proof the dough according to the instructions set forth in the "Proofing" portion of section 2 (pages 108–112). The dough should be uncovered and proofed until the Pullman pan is about ¾ full. The dough will proof about 1 1/2 to 2 inches above the edge of a standard 1.5 pound loaf pan. Proofing should take approximately 45–60 minutes, or until the dough springs back to the touch. If the dough remains dented after lightly touching it, continue proofing the dough until it springs back.
8. If you are using a Pullman pan, oil the lid and slide it onto the pan (if not, leave the loaf pan as is). Bake the dough at 375°F for approximately 40 minutes (but remember, this may change, depending

Pain de mie in Pullman pan.

on altitude and your oven). Because steam is not being used, there is no need to vent. The crust should be golden brown. (Because you can't see the crust on the loaf in the Pullman pan, when the time gets close to the end, slide the lid back and look at it to see if it appears done.) You can also take the internal temperature of the dough, which should be around 205°F.

9. Remove the bread from its pan and cool the bread according to the instructions set forth in the "Cooling" portion of section 2 (pages 130–131).

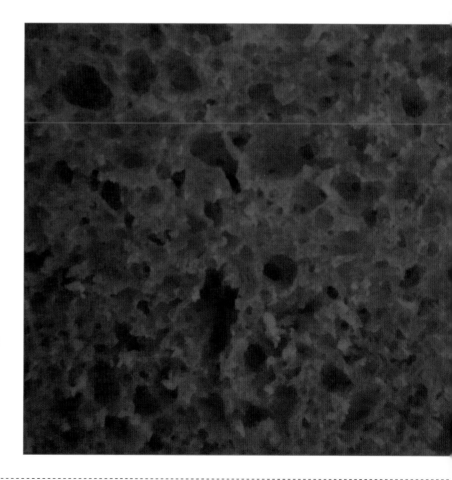

BRIOCHE

Because you have to refrigerate this dough overnight, be sure to take that into consideration when planning out your timing schedule. I can't tell you how many times I decided to make brioche, only to remember that I'd have to wait another whole day to finally bake it. That's disappointment at its finest!

Dough—DDT: 75°F

Makes enough dough for about 526 grams (1.2 pounds) of bread

Ingredient	Weight	Baker's Percentage of Final Dough
Bread Flour	227 grams	100%
Yeast	4 grams	1.8%
Eggs	91 grams	40%
Milk (room temp.)	45 grams	19.8%
Sugar	23 grams	10.1%
Salt	5 grams	2.2%
Butter (medium soft)	136 grams	60%

1. Mix the ingredients, except the butter, according to the instructions in the "Mixing" portion of section 2 (pages 43–44). The butter must be added after the other ingredients are mixed and fully incorporated into one another.

2. To add the butter, follow these instructions (I am going to warn you right now that the dough looks like an absolute disaster for quite a while during this process, but it will shape up in the end. I promise. Just be patient, and keep working on it.):

a. Place the mixed dough in front of you. It will be look rather rough on the surface at this point.

b. Use the conventional kneading technique to make sure that all of the ingredients have been well incorporated into and dispersed throughout the dough.

like the butter is being incorporated into the dough.

c. Place about 1/8 of the butter on top of the dough.

e. Use your scraper to keep all of the ingredients together.

d. Use the conventional kneading technique to blend the butter into the dough. The dough will be extremely soft and moist, and it will not seem

f. Also, because the dough is so sticky, use your scraper to help you fold the dough onto itself while kneading.

eight balls when complete. Note: Because the dough has been refrigerated, it will be very stiff. Although this makes it a bit more difficult to manipulate, it's much better than the dough being too warm, which will cause the butter to melt and the dough to lose all integrity.

> Brioche can also be shaped into a loaf. Just follow the instructions in the "Final Shaping" portion of section 2 (pages 92–93). Bear in mind that the dough will be stiff, so it's going to take a bit of muscle to flatten the dough so that you can shape it into a loaf. But since the internal structure has not yet fully developed, the dough can handle a little-rougher-than-normal treatment.

g. As the butter becomes part of the dough add more butter in 1/8 part increments until all of the butter has been added, and continue kneading. Eventually, the dough will begin to come together. Just keep kneading until the dough is smooth (although it will still be sticky) and it looks well combined. (And if it feels like the dough is becoming too soft, place it in the refrigerator for 15 minutes to chill it. Then pull it out, and begin where you left off.)

3. This dough does not get kneaded per se. In effect, the incorporation of the butter replaces the kneading process.

4. Place the dough in a greased bowl, cover, and refrigerate overnight.

5. Remove the dough from the refrigerator, and, following the instruction in the "Final Shaping" portion of section 2 pages 84–85), shape the dough into small rounds (65 grams each). You should have

6. Grease a 1.5 pound loaf pan, then line the dough in two rows of four balls in the pan.

7. Proof the dough according to the instructions set forth in the "Proofing" portion of section 2 (pages 108–112). The dough should be covered and for approximately 1 to 2 hours (or more if you your kitchen is cooler than 75°F; one way to speed this process along is to utilize the home version of the proofing cabinet, discussed earlier) until the dough has just about doubled or until the dough springs back to the touch. If

much longer for the internal temperature of the dough to rise to the correct level, thus prolonging proofing time.

the dough remains dented after lightly touching it, continue proofing the dough until it springs back. Note: Because the dough has been refrigerated, it takes

8. Brush the top of the dough with an egg wash and bake the dough at 375°F for approximately 30–35 minutes (but remember, this may change depending on altitude and your oven). Because steam is not being used, there is no need to vent. The crust should be golden brown. You can also take the internal temperature of the dough, which should be around 205°F.

9. Remove the bread from its pan and cool the bread according to the instructions set forth in the "Cooling" portion of section 2 (pages 130–131).

CHALLAH

Because of the braiding process involved with this dough, ist's a fun one to make. Just remember that it does not rise during proofing as dramatically as other dough; it's much more subtle, but it still gets ample oven spring.

Dough—DDT: 78°F

Makes enough dough for about 908 grams (2 pounds) of bread

Ingredient	Weight	Baker's Percentage of Final Dough
Bread Flour	500 grams	100%
Yeast	7 grams	1.4%
Water	195 grams	39%
Egg Yolks	95 grams	19%
Vegetable Oil	50 grams	10%
Sugar	50 grams	10%
Salt	9 grams	1.8%

1. Mix the ingredients according to the instructions in the "Mixing" portion of section 2 (pages 43–44). I prefer to beat the eggs before adding them to the rest of the ingredients as I find it helps to evenly disperse them throughout the dough.

2. Knead according to the instructions in the "Kneading Instructions" section 2 (pages 48–49). Because this dough has a low hydration, I recommend using the conventional kneading technique. This may take from 10 to 15 minutes of kneading, depending on how fast and deliberate you are. Because of the low hydration, this dough will not be able to pass the window test. So just make sure that the dough appears smooth and it's clear that all of the ingredients have been thoroughly incorporated into the dough.

3. Bulk ferment the dough according to the instructions in "Bulk Fermentation" portion of section 2 (page 59). Bulk ferment for about 60 minutes or until the dough has just about doubled.

4. Divide the dough into three equal parts (use that scale!). Then following the instructions set forth in the "Preshaping" portion of section 2 (pages 78–79), shape the dough into oblongs.

5. After preshaping, let the dough rest for 15–20 minutes.

6. Using the instructions outlined in the "Final Shaping" portion of section 2 (pages 93–97), form your pieces of dough into strands and then braid the strands together.

7. Grease a baking sheet and dust it with cornmeal as this not only helps to prevent the dough from sticking to the sheet during baking but also adds a nice flavor dimension. (However, if you don't like cornmeal, feel free to omit this step.) You can also use greased parchment paper to line the sheet pan. Proof the dough according to the instructions set forth in the "Proofing" portion of section

2 (pages 108–112). The dough should be covered and proofed for approximately 60 minutes, or until the dough springs back to the touch. If the dough remains dented after lightly touching it, continue proofing the dough until it springs back.

8. Brush the surface—and I mean the top, sides, and all the nooks—with an egg wash then bake the dough at 350°F for approximately 20 minutes (but remember, this may change depending on altitude and your oven). Because steam is not being used, there is no need to vent. The crust should be golden brown. You'll also see great expansion of the dough at the intersections of the braids. You can also take the internal temperature of the dough, which should be around 205°F.

9. Remove the bread from the sheet pan, and cool the bread according to the instructions set forth in the "Cooling" portion of section 2 (pages 130–131).

Sourdough

Sourdough is a naturally leavened bread, which means that yeast is not added to the dough. Rather, a mixture of flour-and-water are allowed to ferment (with some

manipulation) over the course of four to five days. During that time, yeasts that exist in the air infiltrate the flour and water mixture to produce what's called a sourdough starter. That starter is then developed further to produce what baker's call a "leaven." The leaven is then incorporated into the final dough.

Now, it doesn't take too much poking around to realize that there are almost as many sourdough recipes in existence as there are bakers. But after an examination of many of the experts' recipes, along with more than enough trial and error, I've settled on the recipes below—one for white wheat and one for whole wheat sourdough. Not only will these produce wonderful results as is, they allow for room to tweak the whole wheat flour and water contents to create a perfect loaf for your taste. But, as always, start with these recipes and then slowly implement changes. This way you won't have to commit the unforgivable sin in the baker's world—throwing out bread because you were overzealous in attempting to change it.

Sourdough Starter

Makes enough starter for about 908 grams (2 pounds) of bread

Ingredient	Weight	Baker's Percentage of Starter
Bread Flour	100 grams	100%
Water	100 grams	100%

1. Mix the ingredients together. They will resemble a loose batter. (If you haven't noticed already, this is the precise recipe for a *poolish*—equal weights of flour to water.)

2. Place the starter in a covered container, and let it sit at room temperature for one to two days (possibly three days) until the starter begins to bubble. The time it takes depends on the temperature of the room, but 65°F is ideal. You'll know the starter is developing because it will begin to smell sour. Also, starter is a sticky mess, so if it looks anything of the sort, you're making it right.

3. When it has begun to bubble, discard 75 percent of the starter (by weight), then add another 100 grams of water and 100 grams of flour. Twelve or so hours later, you'll notice lots and lots of bubbles on the surface and increase in the overall volume of the starter.

4. Repeat step 3 for the following three days. (By the end, the starter will be developing for five to six days).

5. The starter is now ready to be developed into a leaven for incorporating into the dough.

Sourdough recipes like these, which are higher in water content, are tough to work with. There's no question about it. Just be patient and put in your best effort; the results will be worth it.

Sourdough—DDT: 78°F

(Makes enough dough for about 908 grams (2 pounds) of bread.)

White Wheat Dough

Ingredient	Weight	Baker's Percentage of Final Dough
Bread Flour	440 grams	73.3%
Whole Wheat Flour	60 grams	10%
Water	380 grams	63.3%
Leaven	200 grams	33.3%
Salt	13 grams	2.1%

Whole Wheat Dough

Ingredient	Weight	Baker's Percentage of Starter
Bread Flour	300 grams	50%
Whole Wheat Flour	200 grams	33.3%
Water	380 grams	80%
Leaven	200 grams	33.3%
Salt	13 grams	2.1%

Note: Because there is more whole wheat flour in this recipe, the hydration level has been increased to 80 percent to accommodate this.

1. After choosing one of the above recipes, create the leaven by discarding 75

You'll notice that the white dough recipe includes some whole wheat flour. You can substitute bread flour for the whole wheat flour; however, the whole wheat flour adds a nice dimension in terms of taste and texture, and is commonly incorporated in white wheat sourdough recipes.

percent of the starter then adding 100 grams of flour and 100 grams of water to remaining 25 percent of the starter. Allow this to sit at room temperature for 12 hours. At the end of the 12 hours, your leaven is ready to go. Just be sure not to add all of the leaven to the final dough recipe; instead, add only the 200 grams called for. You can then add 100 grams of water and 100 grams of flour to it to feed it (leaven and starter need food to live) to keep it alive for the next use. Be sure to feed the starter every one to two weeks to keep it alive. And place it in your refrigerator after feeding to preserve it for your next bake.

2. Mix the water, bread flour, wheat flour, and leaven until they are thoroughly combined. Do not add the salt because it will tighten the gluten strands, which is precisely the opposite of what you'd like to accomplish here. The dough will be extremely sticky, and you won't be able

to work with it in any effective manner. For the dough to develop into a workable form, you will have to utilize what's called an "autolyse," which is essential for gluten development in naturally leavened bread. To do this, cover the mixture so it doesn't form a skin on top and allow it to sit for up to an hour—the closer you can get to an hour the better. This will allow the flour to absorb the water, which in turn will allow the gluten to develop—all without doing a thing. And after an hour, the dough will firm up. The autolyse reduces mixing time and increases the extensibility (its tendency to retract to its original state) of the dough. It also improves flavor and the texture of the crumb. Note: The dough is still going to be wet after the autolyse. If you feel it's still too wet, allow the autolyse to rest a bit longer before moving on to the next step. Also, you can remove the cover; that will allow some of the moisture to evaporate. But do so only as a last resort—most likely in a very humid climate—because you don't want to decrease the hydration level in the process.

Autolyse: dough after mixing, but before rest. Notice how sticky the dough is.

Autolyse: dough after one hour of rest. Notice how much smoother the dough is. You can see how elastic it is by the way it stretches around my finger.

3. Mix in the salt. To do this you'll have to knead the dough rather well. I prefer to do this while it's still in its mixing bowl. Just make sure you blend in the salt so that it's well dispersed throughout the dough. Then use the French kneading method—maybe a dozen or so times—to bring it all together. When you start to see bubbles forming on the surface, move on to the next step. Remember, this is a wet dough, so you're never going to get it to come together that well; it's always going to be sticky. Just be patient and let the rest of the steps take care of that.

4. Cover the dough and let it bulk ferment according to the instructions in the Bulk Fermentation portion of Section 2 (page 59) for 45 minutes and fold. (Because the dough will be so sticky at first, I recommend using the second method of folding dough. It's a bit easier to manage. And you will definitely need to use your bench scraper because the dough will be very, very wet at first.) Ferment 45 more minutes and fold.

Ferment yet another 30 minutes and fold. Ferment another 30 minutes and fold. Then ferment for a final 30 minutes. This amounts to three hours of bulk fermentation, so plan accordingly.

5. Following the instructions set forth in the "Preshaping" portion of section 2 (pages 76–79), shape the dough into an oblong (if you want a *batard*) or a round (if you want a *boule*).

6. After preshaping, let the dough rest for 15–20 minutes.

7. Using the instructions outlined in the "Final Shaping" portion of section 2 (pages 83–91), form the dough into either a *batard* or round.

8. Proof the dough according to the instructions set forth in the "Proofing" portion of section 2 (pages 108–112). A *batard* can be proofed either on a peel or in an oval *banneton* topside down. A round can be proofed either on a peel or in a round *banneton* topside down. (*Bannetons* work wonders for proofing sourdough, so don't hesitate to use one if you have one on hand.) The dough should be covered and proofed for approximately 1 to 1 1/2 hours. The dough should spring back to the touch. If the dough remains dented after lightly touching it, continue proofing the dough until it springs back.

9. Remove the dough from the *bannetons*, if you've used them, and place them on a peel. (If you proofed the dough on a peel, leave it right where it is.) Score the dough according to the instructions set forth in the "Scoring" portion of section 2 (pages 113–114). Note: Because this is a very wet dough, the razor or *lame* has a tendency to drag across the dough. Also, remember that the whole wheat dough will not open up as much upon scoring or in the oven because of the hulls, which tend to cut the gluten strands within the dough.

10. Place your dough in the oven and steam the oven according to the instructions set forth in the "Baking" portion of section 2 (page 126).

11. Bake the dough at 470°F for approximately 35–40 minutes (but remember, this may change depending on altitude and your oven). Remember to vent the oven during the final 10 minutes of baking. Test for doneness by using a thermometer or thumping the bottom of the loaf. You can also listen for that crackling sound if you place it close to your ear. The crust should be golden brown.

Because sourdough starter has had time to ferment and develop flavor, you will find that some recipes call for shorter bulk fermentation of the final dough. This is perfectly acceptable. Nevertheless, a prolonged bulk fermentation will definitely improve the flavor—no question about it.

Once you bake your sourdough, leave it out in the air overnight. This will help the crust get nice and hard, and allowing it to rest before eating it will allow the bread to attain its maximum flavor potential.

THE BAKER'S PERCENTAGE

Before I leave you, I cannot fail to address—or, quite frankly, avoid—talking about the often dreaded concept of the baker's percentage. I would be doing neither you nor myself justice without its inclusion. I placed it here—at the very end—because I discovered that the baker's percentage is much easier to understand once you've looked through, and possibly worked through, some or all of the recipes covered above. I will warn you right now, though, that the math below appears maddening at first glance, but I will also assure you that if you take the time to study it, you'll soon see that the calculations are wholly useful when you decide that it's time you start making these recipes your own by tweaking them to your liking. What's more, it's perfectly logical and not all that difficult to comprehend and put into use once you do the math yourself a few times.

So, what exactly is the baker's percentage?

In a nutshell, the baker's percentage is simply the ratio of different ingredients to each other in a recipe. These ratios allow a baker to increase or decrease a recipe and still achieve the same end result, and it permits a baker to readily assess the nature of a recipe, which will give the baker an idea of exactly what the end product will look and taste like. Although many bread-baking books fail to address this topic in this way, the ratios are still there. I think that the authors just don't want to scare anyone off. But the fact is that knowledge is power when it comes to understanding baker's percentages.

Once you understand the baker's percentage, you'll be able to follow in the footsteps of many artisan bakers and manipulate the hydration levels in your straight dough, prefermented dough, and sourdough to achieve those really cool large and glossy holes in your bread—particularly baguettes and sourdough. However, if you choose to do so, tackle this in incremental stages of no more than 2–2.5 percent increase by weight at a time. (These values will become crystal clear as you advance through this section. And I've found that if you have a context in which to incorporate the baker's percentages, it makes them much simpler to comprehend, and hydration level is a perfect context to use.) If you increase it too fast, the potential for failing miserable increases exponentially.

Let's look at a sample recipe to see how this all works:

Bread Flour	1000 grams
Water	700 grams
Salt	20 grams
Yeast	10 grams

Now that we've got some numbers, we can understand how they relate to each other.

The foundation of the baker's percentage is the weight of the flour. Flour is articulated as 100 percent, and it is the number upon which all of the other ratios are based (i.e., all ingredients are represented as a percentage of the weight of the flour). So, the baker's percentages for this recipe are the following:

Bread Flour	100% (1,000 [the weight of the flour] is the percentage against which all others are formulated)
Water	70% (700 [the weight of the water] divided by 1000 [the weight of the flour])
Salt	2% (20 [the weight of the salt] divided by 1000 [the weight of the flour])
Yeast	1% (10 [the weight of the yeast] divided by 1000 [the weight of the flour])

This means that the ratio of flour to water, salt, and yeast is 100% to 70%, 20%, and 10%, respectively. What effect does this have on bread baking? Well, say a recipe only gives you weights but no baker's percentages and you want to calculate the hydration level (or the ratio of flour to water in the recipe) to see how wet the dough will be before mixing it. By knowing that you divide the weight of the water by the weight of the flour, you can make this determination (and the same goes for the rest of the ingredients).

Using percentages also allows you to increase or decrease a recipe. For example, let's say that you have 800 grams of flour left in your bag and want to use it all up on this recipe. All you have to do is multiply the baker's percentages by the 800 gram weight of the flour. Here's what the modified recipe will look like:

Bread Flour	800 grams (800 [the weight of the flour] multiplied by 100% [the baker's percentage of the flour])
Water	560 grams (800 [the weight of the flour] multiplied by 70% [the baker's percentage of water])
Salt	16 grams (800 [the weight of the flour] multiplied by 2% [the baker's percentage of salt])
Yeast	8 grams (800 [the weight of the flour] multiplied by 1% [the baker's percentage of yeast])

This same math can be used to increase or decrease the size of the same recipe. Here's how to do it:

1) Determine how much weight of dough your recipe will produce by adding together the weights of all the ingredients (1000 + 700 + 20 + 10 = 1,730 grams of dough [about 3.8 pounds of dough]);
2) Add all of the baker's percentages for the recipe together (100 + 70 + 2 + 1 = 173%);
3) Determine how many pounds of dough you'd like to create (let's use 2,270 grams [or 5 pounds of dough]);
4) Divide the desired weight by the total of the baker's percentages to achieve the multiplying factor (2,270 divided by 173 = 13.12);
5) Multiply the multiplying factor by the weight percentage of each ingredient and then multiply by 100 to arrive at the new weight of the recipe:

Bread Flour	1312 grams (13.12 [the multiplying factor] multiplied by 100% [the baker's percentage of flour] multiplied by 100)
Water	918 grams (rounded) (13.12 [the multiplying factor] multiplied by 70% [the baker's percentage of water] multiplied by 100)
Salt	26 grams (rounded) (13.12 [the multiplying factor] multiplied by 2% [the baker's percentage of salt] multiplied by 100)
Yeast	13 (rounded) (13.12 [the multiplying factor] multiplied by 1% [the baker's percentage of yeast] multiplied by 100)

This calculation is extremely helpful when you come across institutional-size recipes (i.e., those that call for 50 or 100 pounds of dough) and need to resize them for home use.

Now, here's a twist (isn't there always a twist?). If you use a preferment or sourdough starter in your recipe, you'll need to add the weights of the flour and water (yeast isn't a factor for most preferments made at home because most call for just a pinch, and salt isn't part of a starter so it's not factored in either) in the preferment or starter to the weight of the flour and water in the rest of the recipe to determine the overall weights of all the ingredients. For example, look at the same recipe that incorporates a *biga* (a type of preferment) that results in a 50% baker's percentage in the dough:

Biga

Bread Flour	334 grams (100% baker's percentage)
Water	167 grams (50% baker's percentage, or 167 [the weight of the water] divided by 334 [the weight of the flour])
Yeast	Pinch

Dough

Bread Flour	1000 grams
Water	700 grams
Salt	20 grams
Yeast	10 grams
Biga	501 grams (50% baker's percentage, or 501 [the weight of the flour] divided by 1,000 [the weight of the flour])

As a result, the total weight of the flour is now 1,334 grams, and the total weight of the water is now 867 grams. So, the weights for the entire recipe with the *biga* are the following:

Bread Flour	1,334 grams (1,000 [the weight of the flour in the dough] plus 334 [the weight of the flour in the *biga*])
Water	866 grams (700 [the weight of the water in the dough] plus 166 [the weight of the water in the *biga*])
Salt	20 grams (the same as the recipe since no salt is in the *biga*)
Yeast	10 grams (the same as the recipe since the yeast added to the *biga* is negligible)

And the total baker's percentages are:

Bread Flour	100% (the base percentage [1,344 grams])
Water	65% (867 grams [the weight of the water in the *biga* and dough] divided by 1,344 [the weight of the flour in the *biga* and dough])
Salt	1.5% (20 grams [the weight of salt in the dough] divided by 1,344 [the weight of the flour in the *biga* and dough])
Yeast	.7% (10 grams [the weight of the yeast in the dough] divided by 1,344 [the weight of the flour in the *biga* and dough])

Not that you're going to play with this math all that often, but it does illustrate how much preferments can impact the overall baker's percentages in a formula.

Although this may be the end of the book, it is just the beginning of your career in dough. To lead you on your journey into the flour-covered world of bread baking, I leave you with these thoughts.

It is my sincere hope that:

- you have gained an appreciation of the skill and artistry that the craft of baking bread entails;

- you comprehend all of the concepts contained herein and intend with all your heart to put them to good use;

- you understand that, in the end, there are only two essential ingredients for becoming a baker among bakers— passion and determination; and

- most of all, that you make many mistakes along the way, for out of such misfortunes the greatest of masters are born.

Now, go bake some bread!

Although the vast majority of the ingredients and equipment can be purchased locally, here are a few companies that offer some of the tough to get or highly prized ingredients and equipment:

Flour

Both of these flour mills produce a variety of organic and nut-free flours. I've used both, and they work spectacularly.

Heartland Mill
www.heartlandmill.com
Lehi Roller Mills
www.lehirollermill.com

Equipment

These companies offer some of the tough to find equipment for bread baking:

TMB Baking—*Couches, bannetons, lames,* and much more.
www.tmbbaking
Forno Bravo—Thick baking stones.

www.fornobravo.com
The Restaurant Depot Store—Full array of restaurant supplies, from peels to padded floor mats to containers, and more.
www.therdstore.com

Books

There are dozens upon dozens of useful bread baking books on the market; however, after looking through and using dozens upon dozens of them myself, these are my all-time favorites. Not only do they provide great recipes, but they explain a lot about technique:

Bread: A Baker's Book of Techniques and Recipes by Jeffrey Hamelman
- This is *the* bible of bread baking from a master baker and the head of the King Arthur Flour Bakery. It's an advanced book—PhD-level material—which makes it a great reference guide for someone who has a thorough grasp on the bread-baking process. If I had to pick one

book to have on my shelf at all times, this would be it.

Bread Alone: Bold Fresh Loaves from Your Own Hands by Daniel Leader and Judith Blahnik

- The authors should be commended many times over for their dedication to informing the public about the atrocities inherent in store-bought bread. In addition to offering a multitude of recipes, they provide a healthy dose of information on ingredients and technique. It's a nice addition to your baking book collection that will give you tons of bread to bake and something to think about every time you see a store made loaf of bread.

Baking: Mastering the Art and Craft by the Culinary Institute of America

- From one of the top culinary education institutions, this book puts forth a technical look at baking virtually everything, including a substantial portion on bread baking. It's a great reference book; the only downside to this book is that many of its recipes are institutional-size (i.e., 10 to 90 pounds), so you'll have to put those baker's percentages to work. Other than that, it's always within reach when I'm baking.

The next two books are from some modern bakers, who I think are, without question, at the top of the bread-baking game:

Dough: Simple Contemporary Bread by Richard Bertinet

- Bertinet is a huge proponent of the French kneading method. His recipes are very solid, but what I value most about his book is that it taught me how to be creative with recipes. Take a look at his book, and you'll know what I mean. He's taken baking to a whole new level. Wow! That's all I can say.

Tartine Bread by Chad Robertson

- In my opinion, Robertson is equal parts scientist and artist, and that's one hell of a one-two combination when it comes to bread baking. From the very beginning of this book, you can sense his passion for what he does, and his instructions technically explain the bread-baking process. If you want to get into the mind of a master, read this.

Matt Pellegrini, a lifelong home baker and cook, is the coauthor of *Cowboy: The Ultimate Guide to Living Like a Great American Icon*, which includes an entire chapter on mastering the art of chuck wagon cooking. In addition to a career in writing, Matt has worked as a strength coach, carpenter, litigation attorney, public policy analyst, and many things in between. He spends his time in Colorado and Florida with his cattle dog, Appaloosa.